# Enchanted Forest

## Coloring Book for Adults

✓ **55** adorable **coloring** pages

✓ **Great for aspiring** adults **and** teens

✓ **Ideal for** colored **pencils, markers or colored pencils**

✓ Large **print page** format: **8.5 x 11 inches**

✓ **Single-sided** pages **to avoid spills, ensuring your masterpieces stay clean**

✓ Activity **to help** artists **relax and explore creativity**

✓ Reduces **anxiety**

✓ **Full** page

*vol. 2*

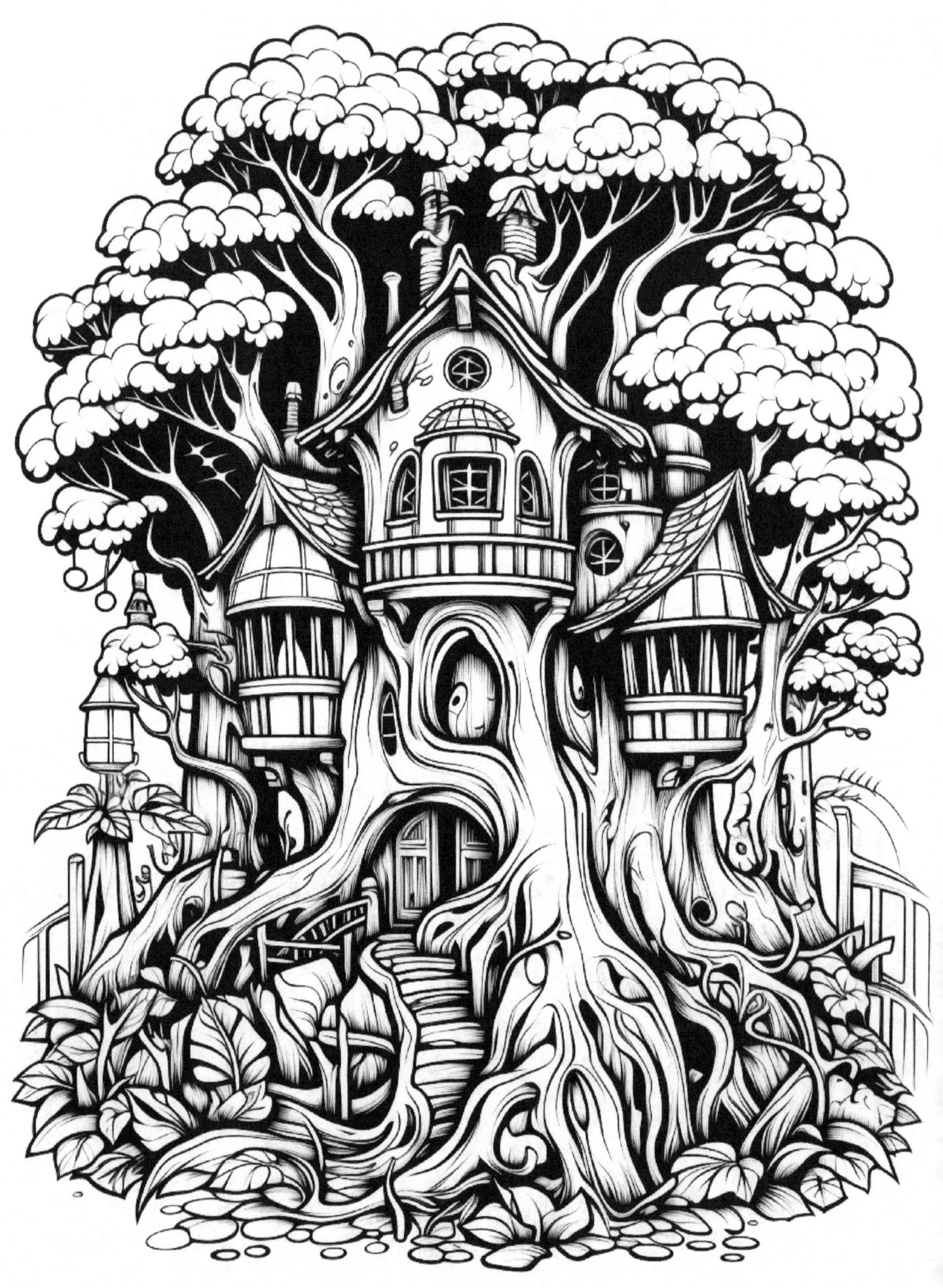

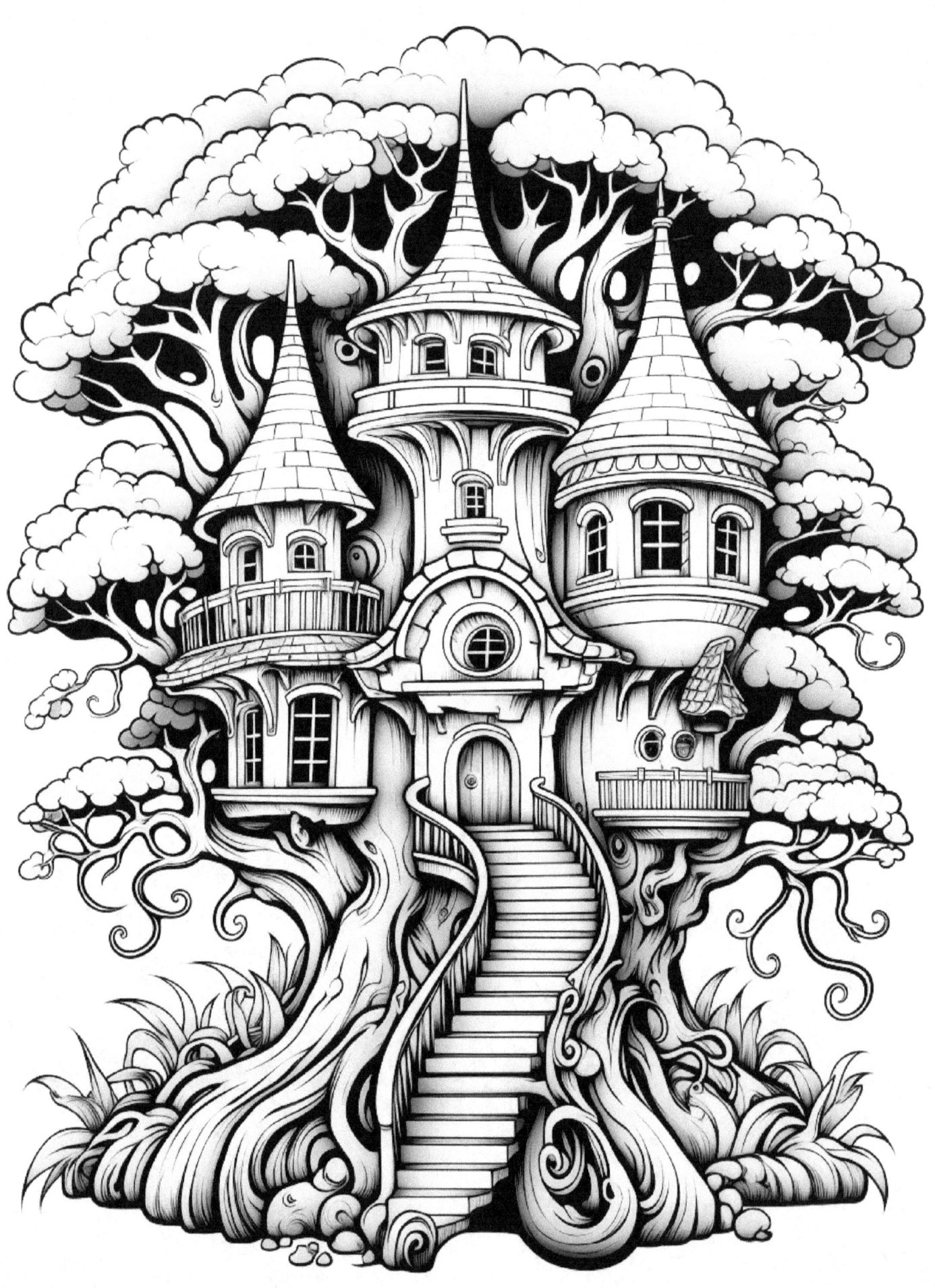

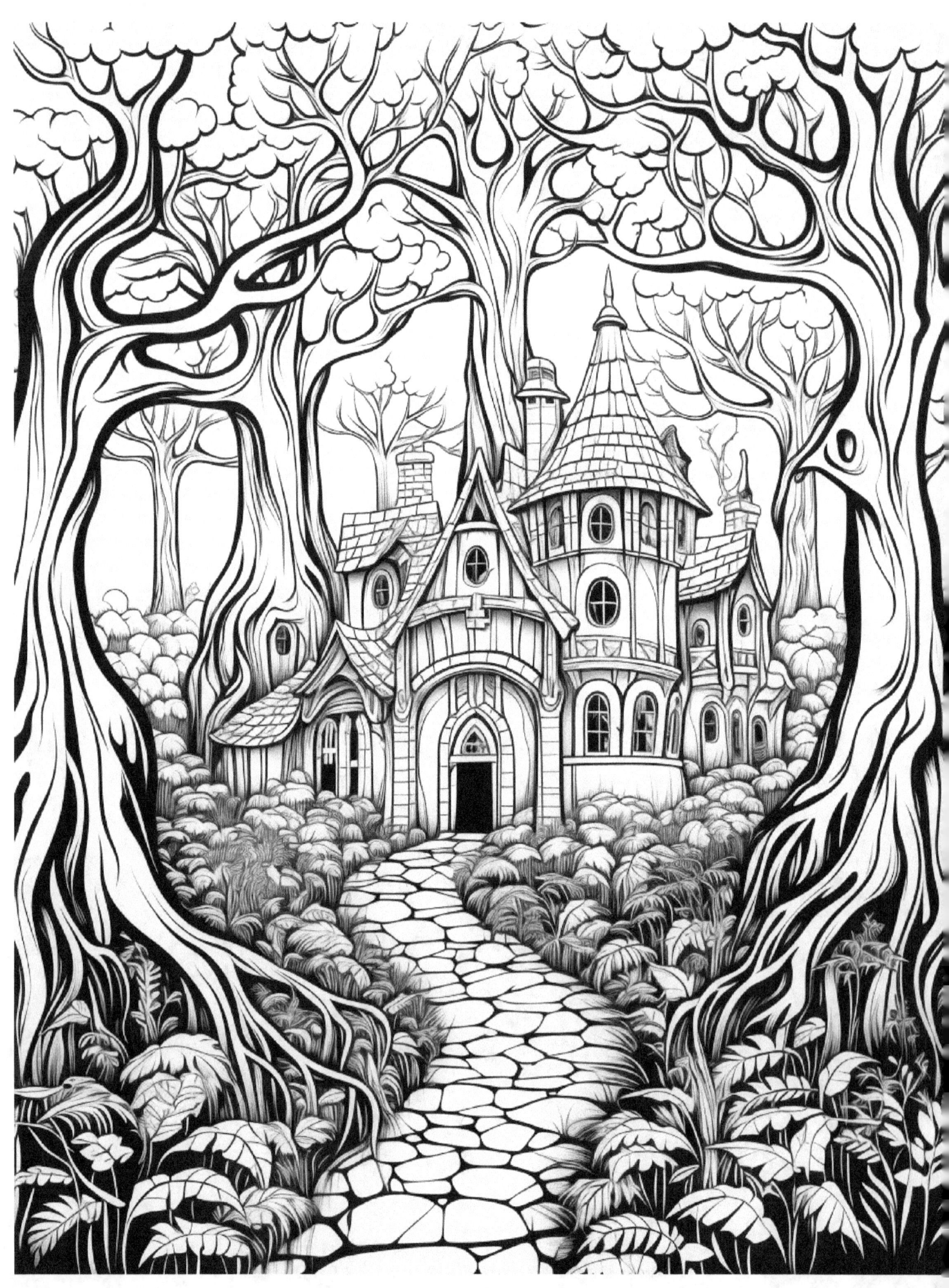

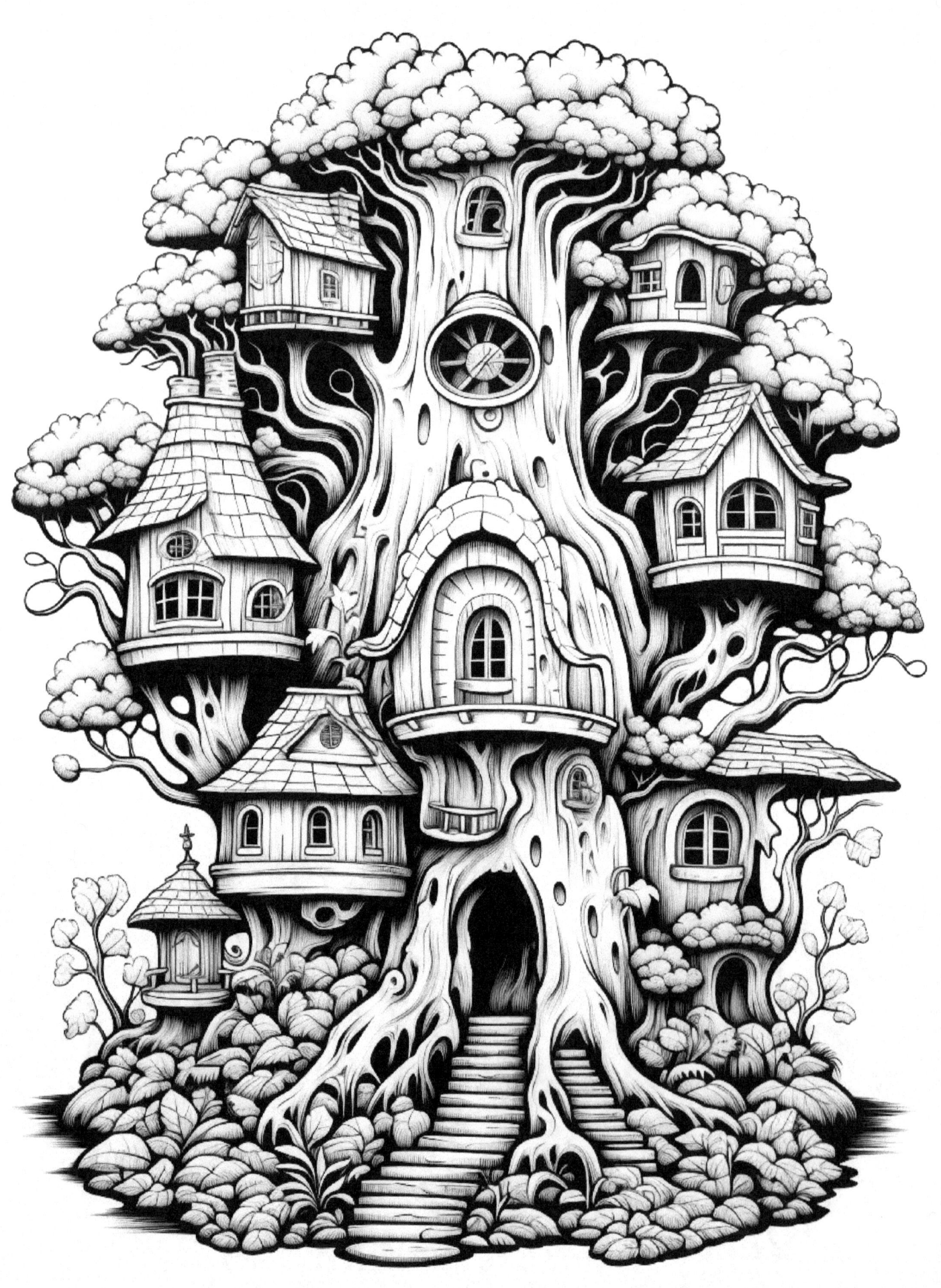

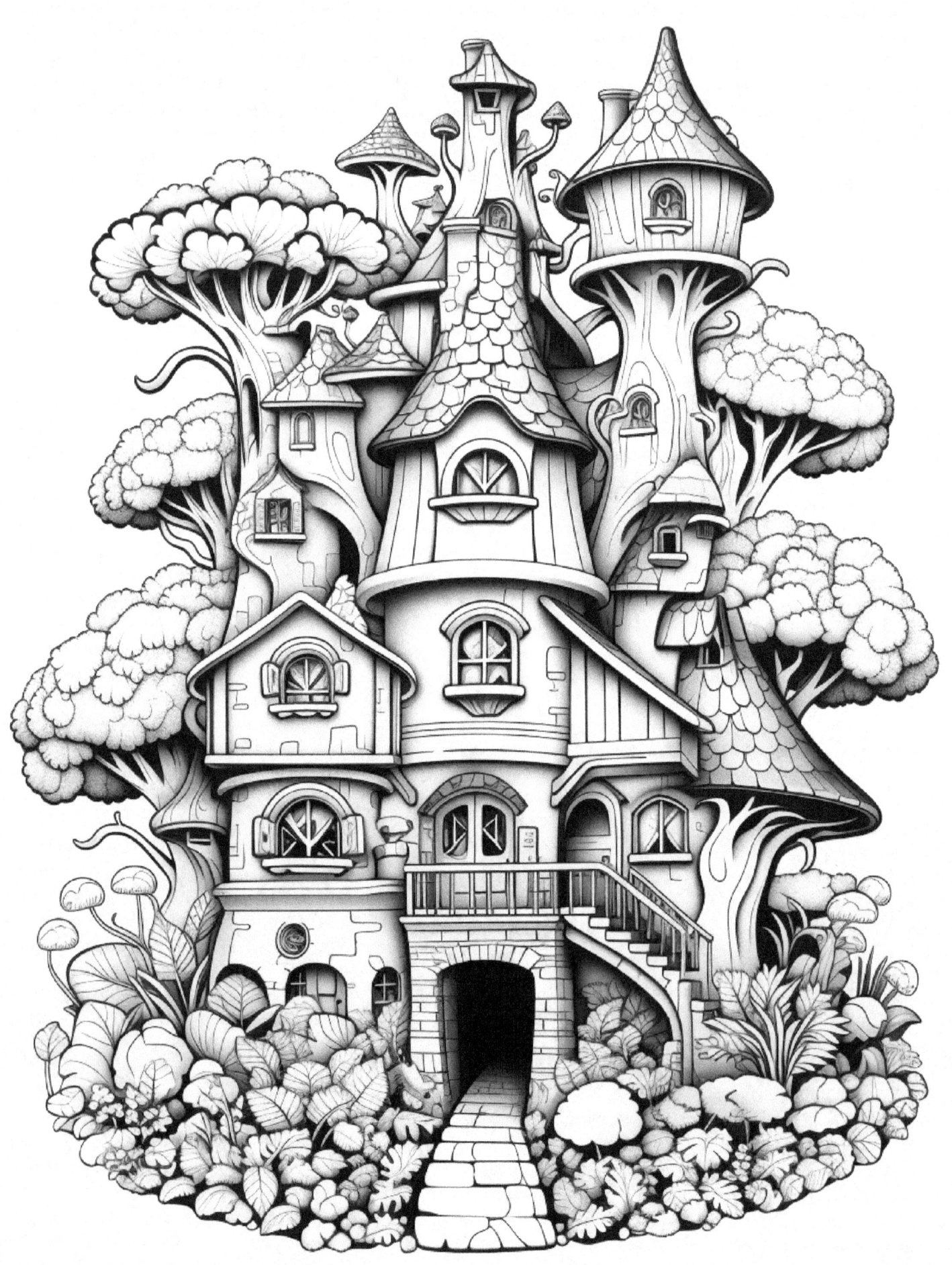

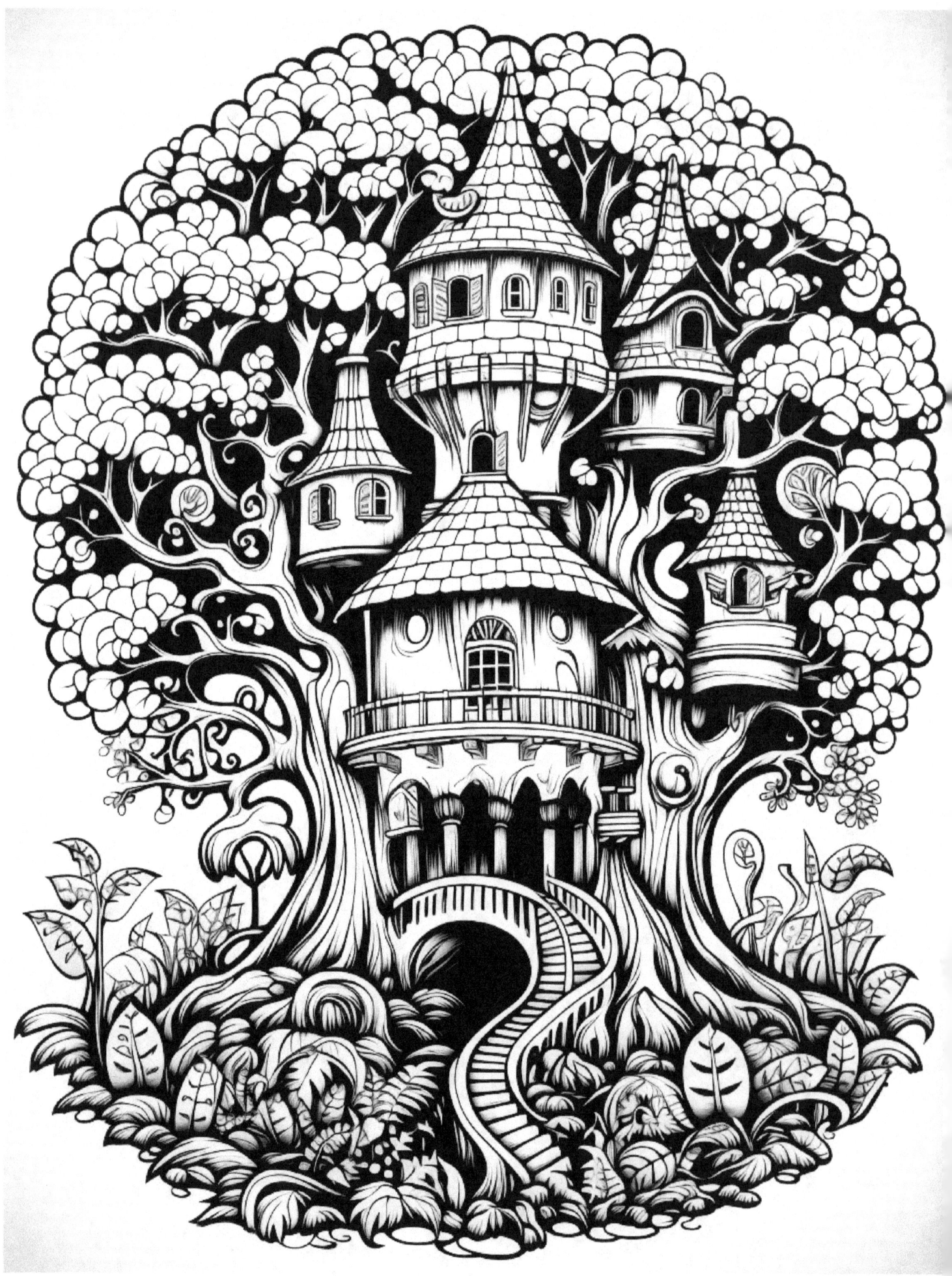

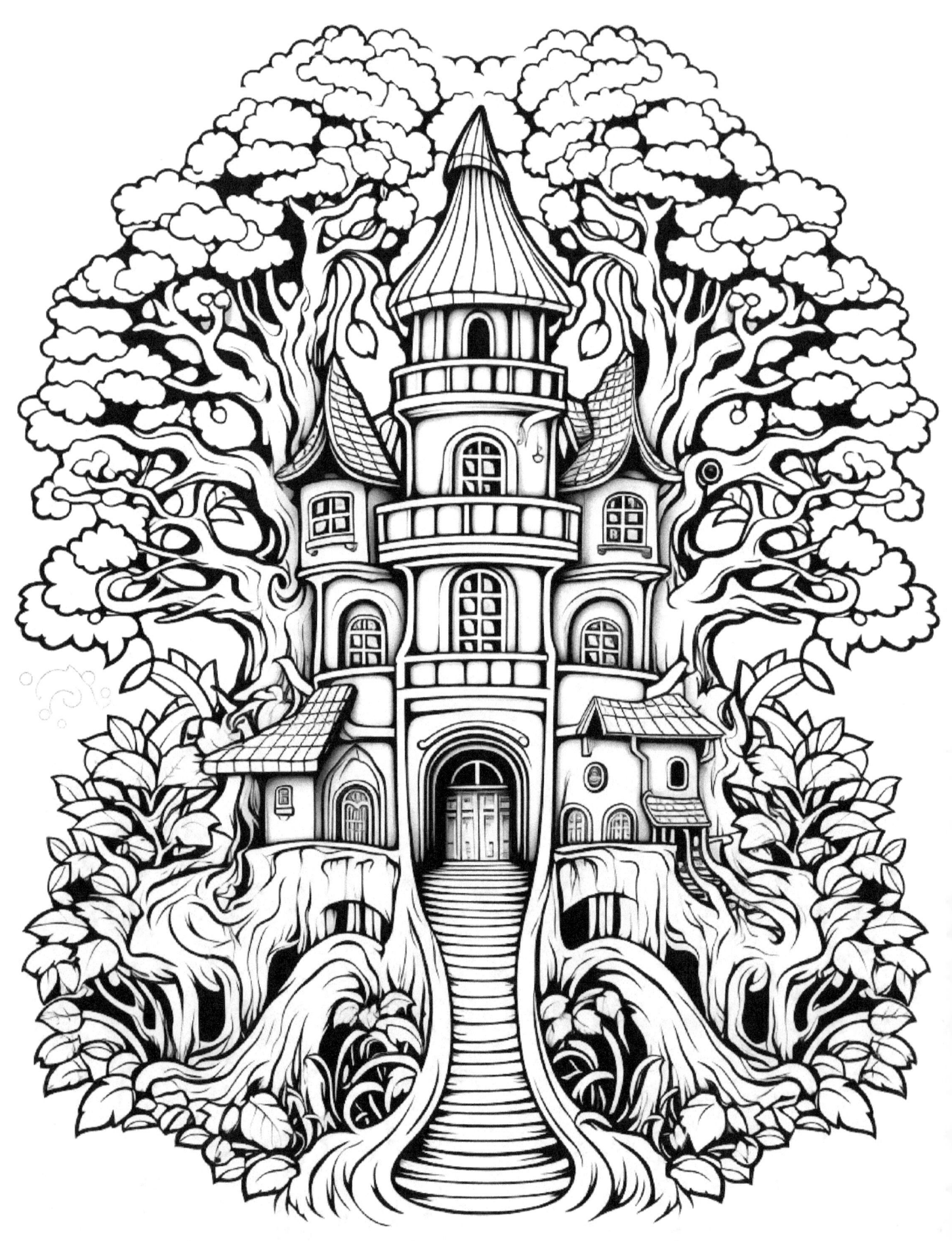

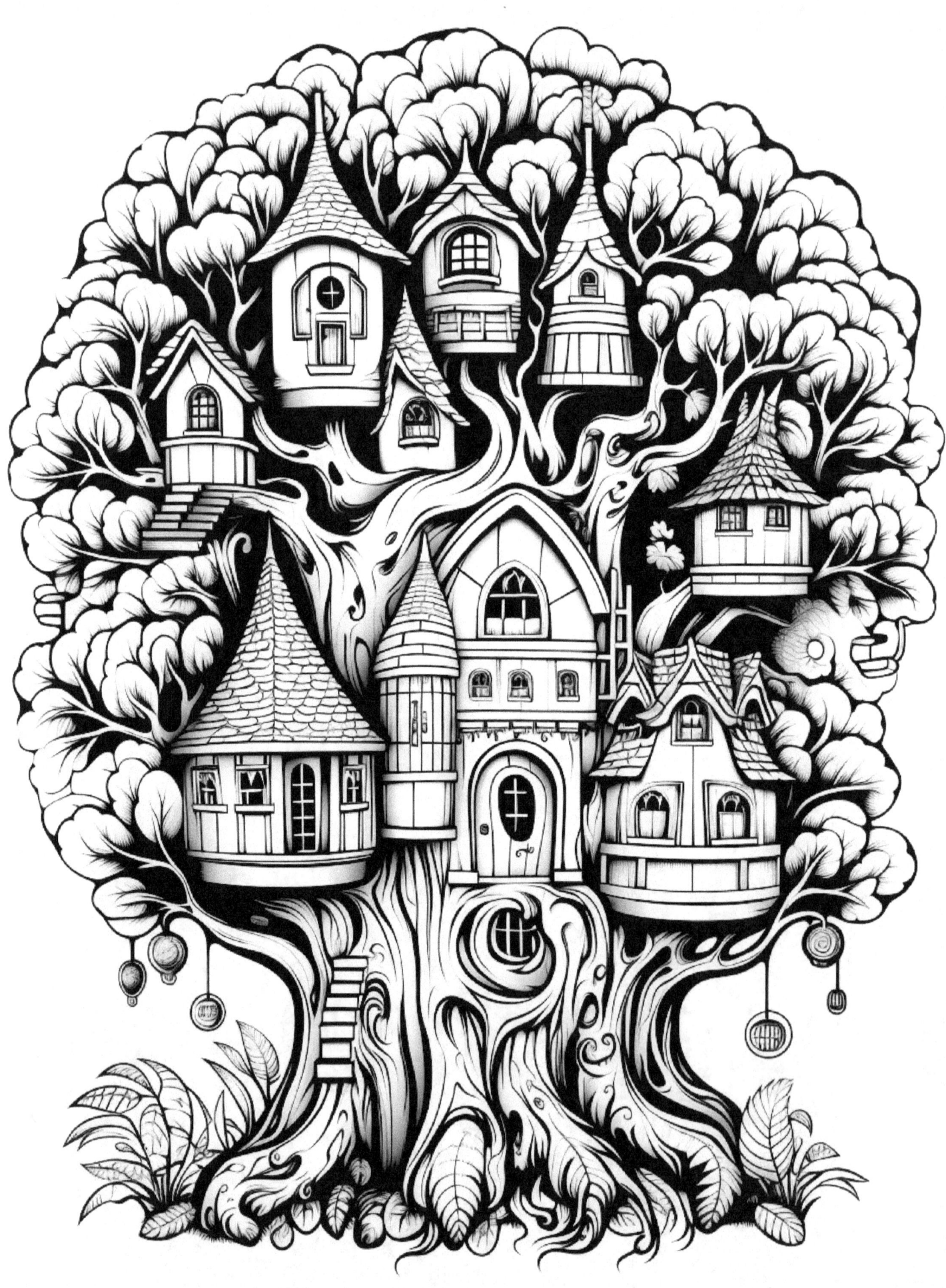

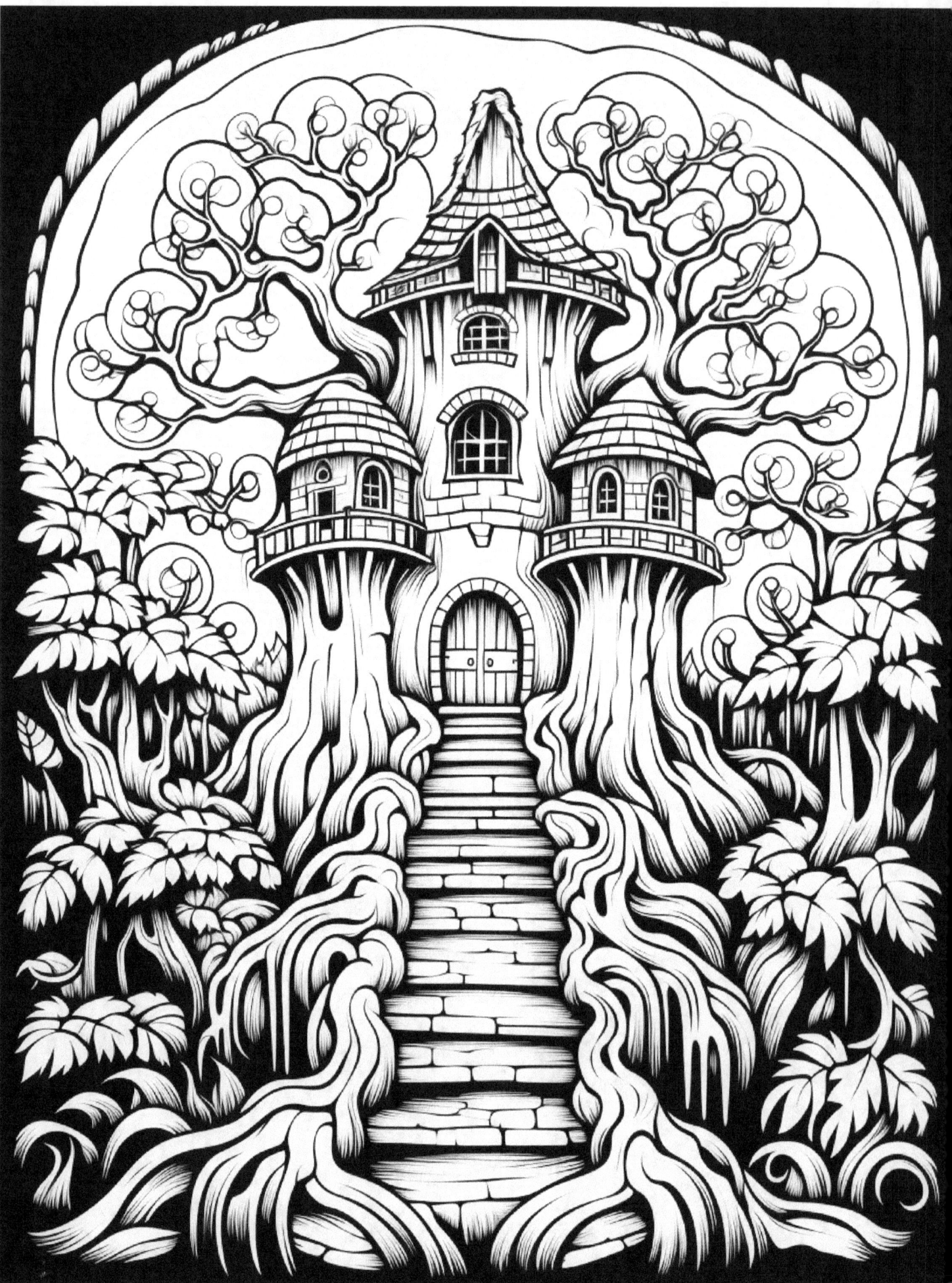

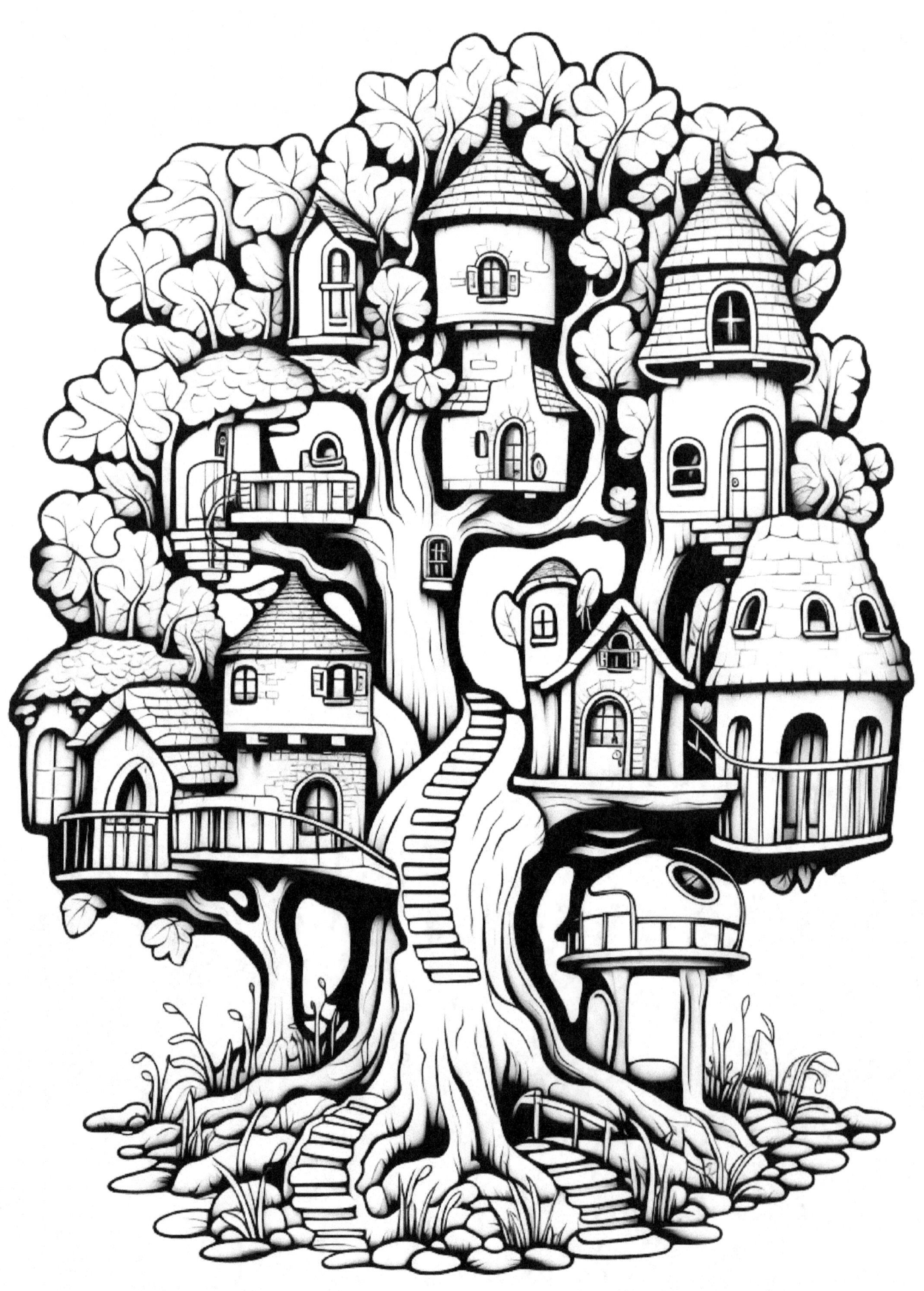

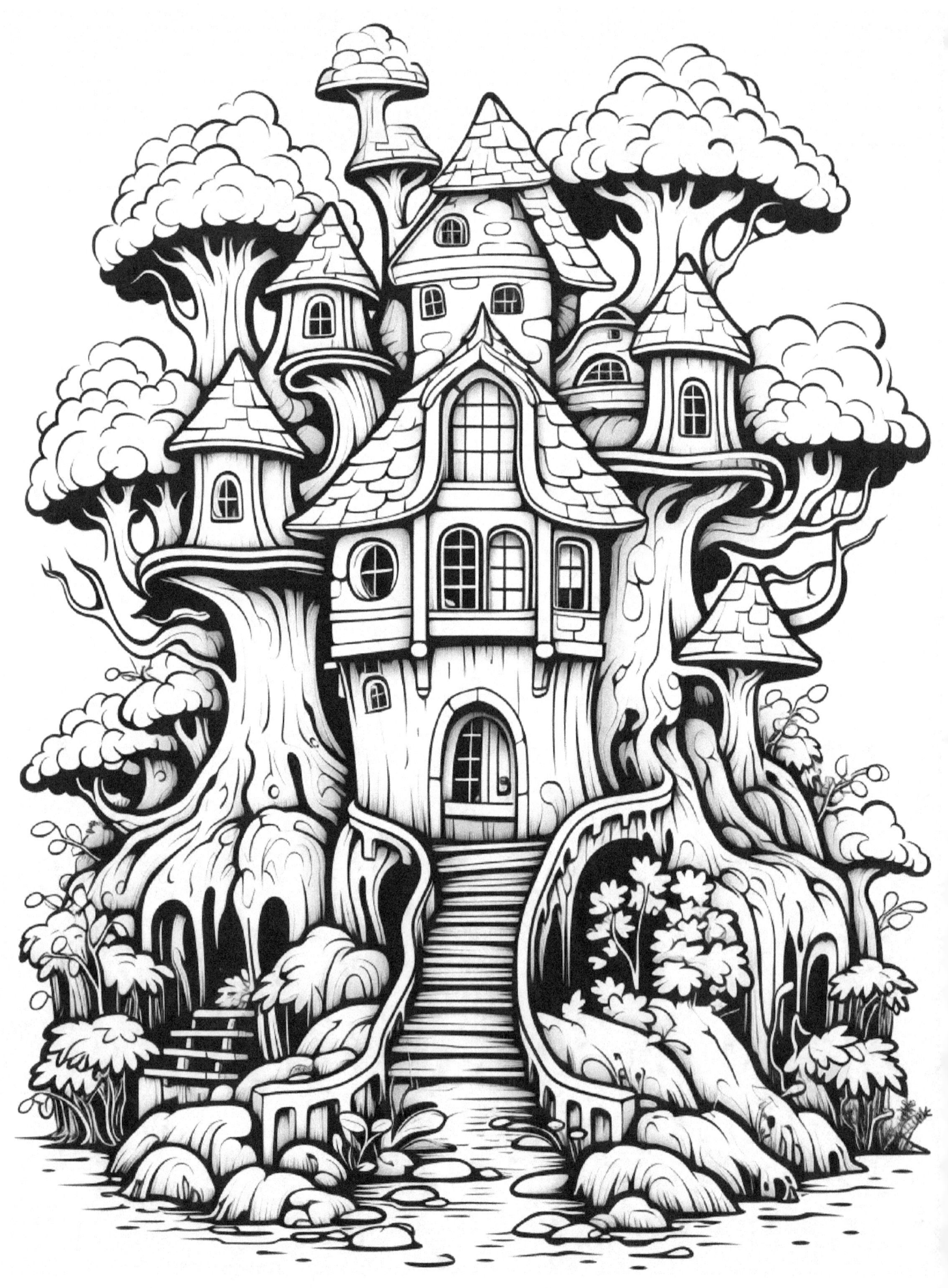

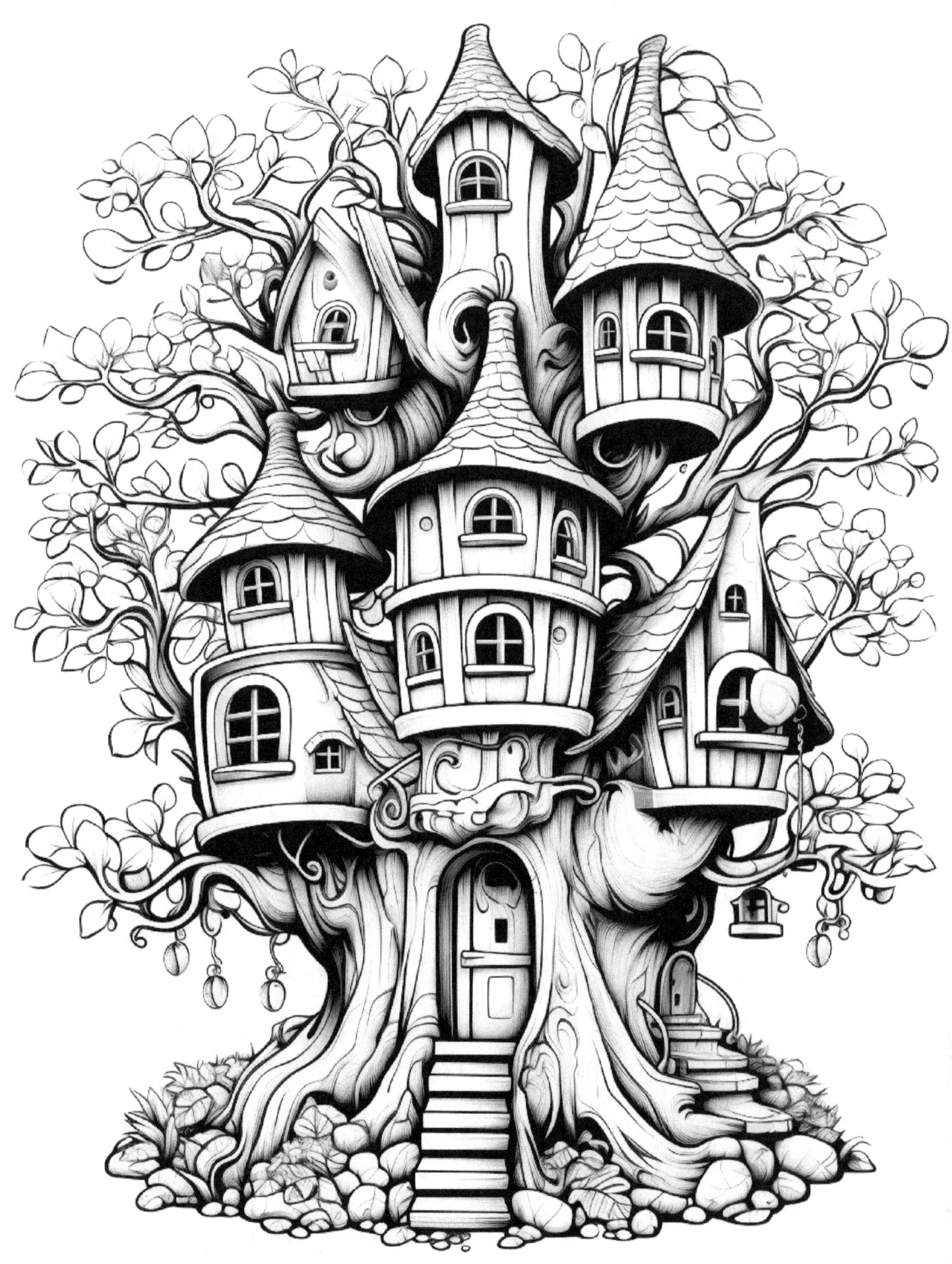

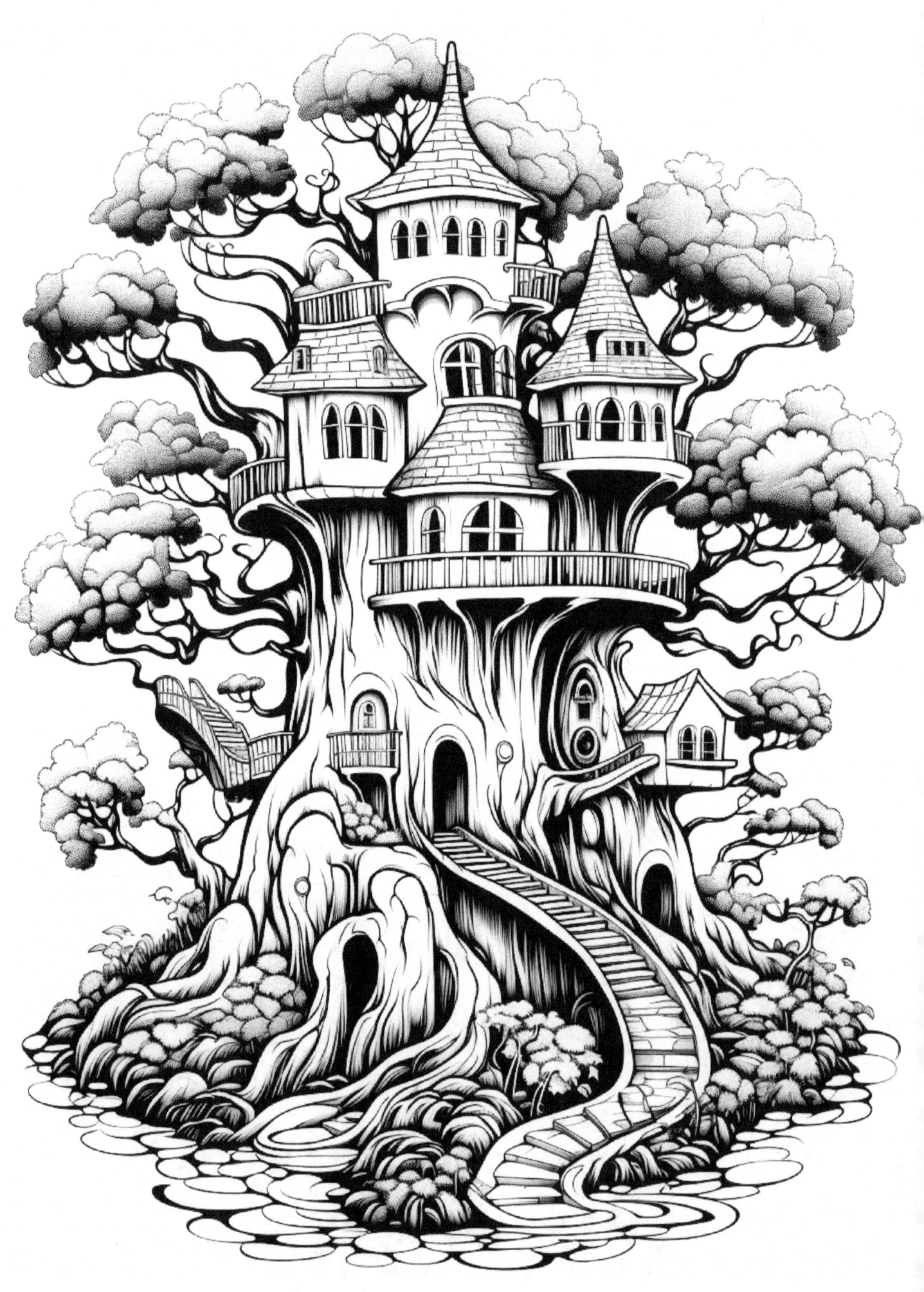

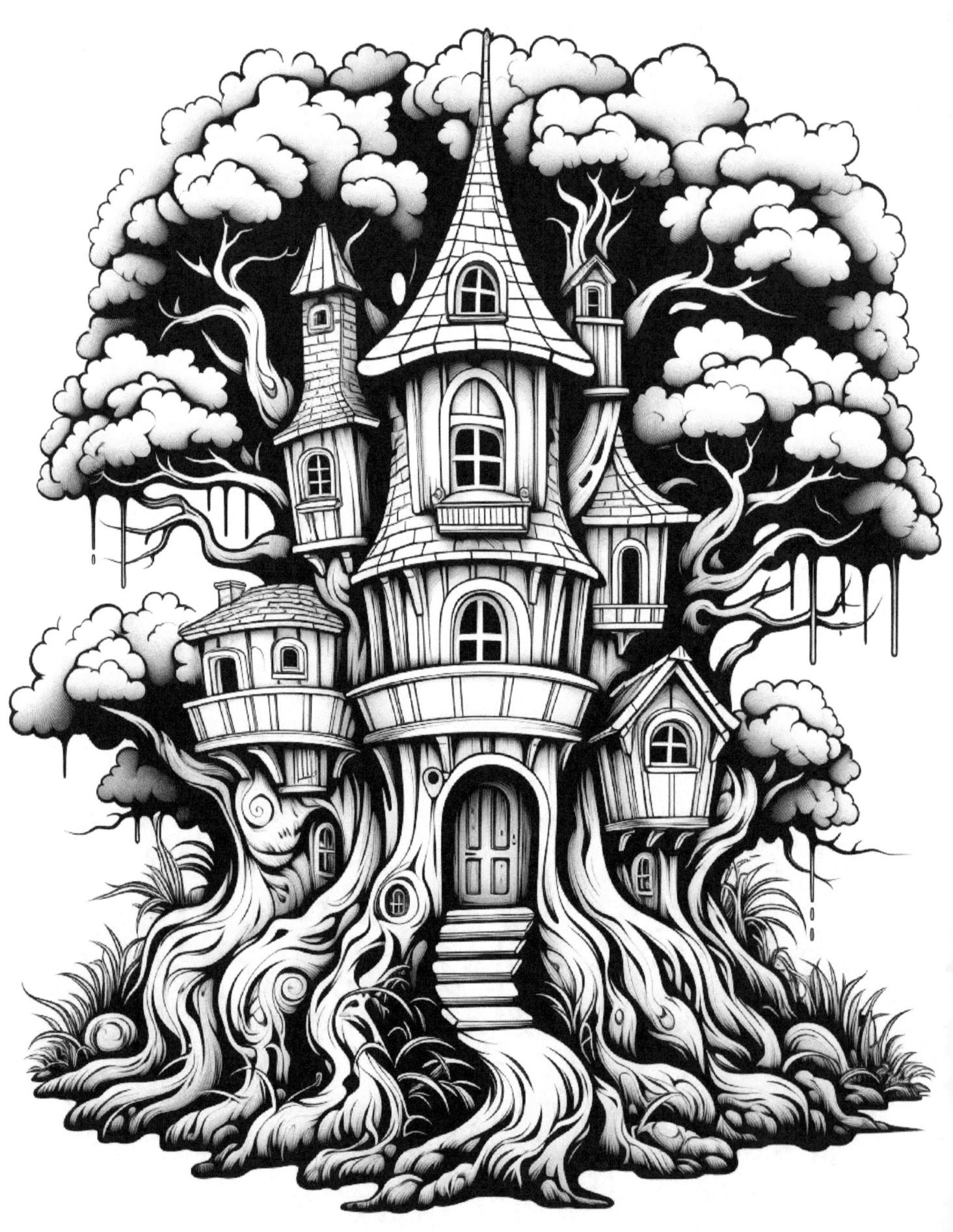

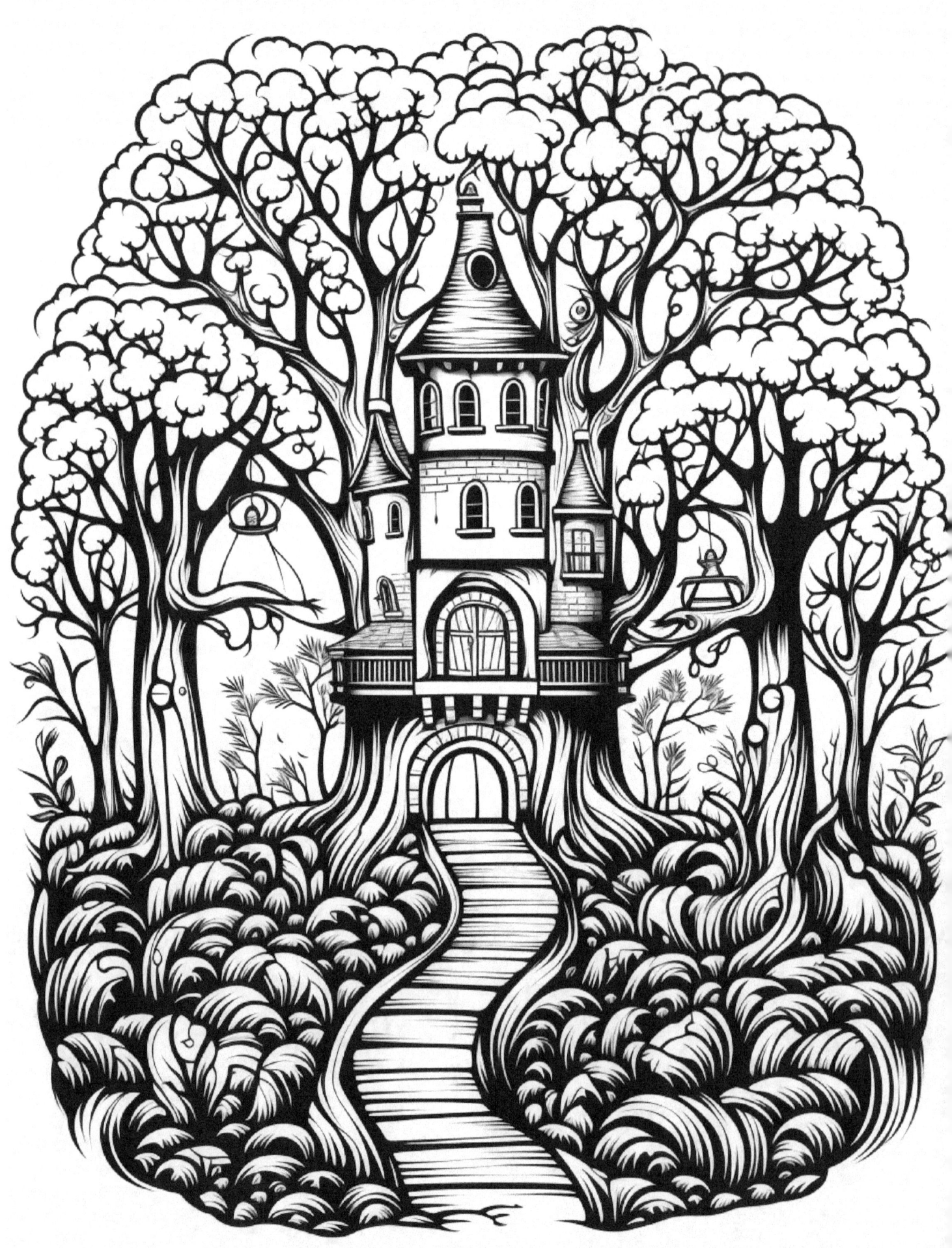

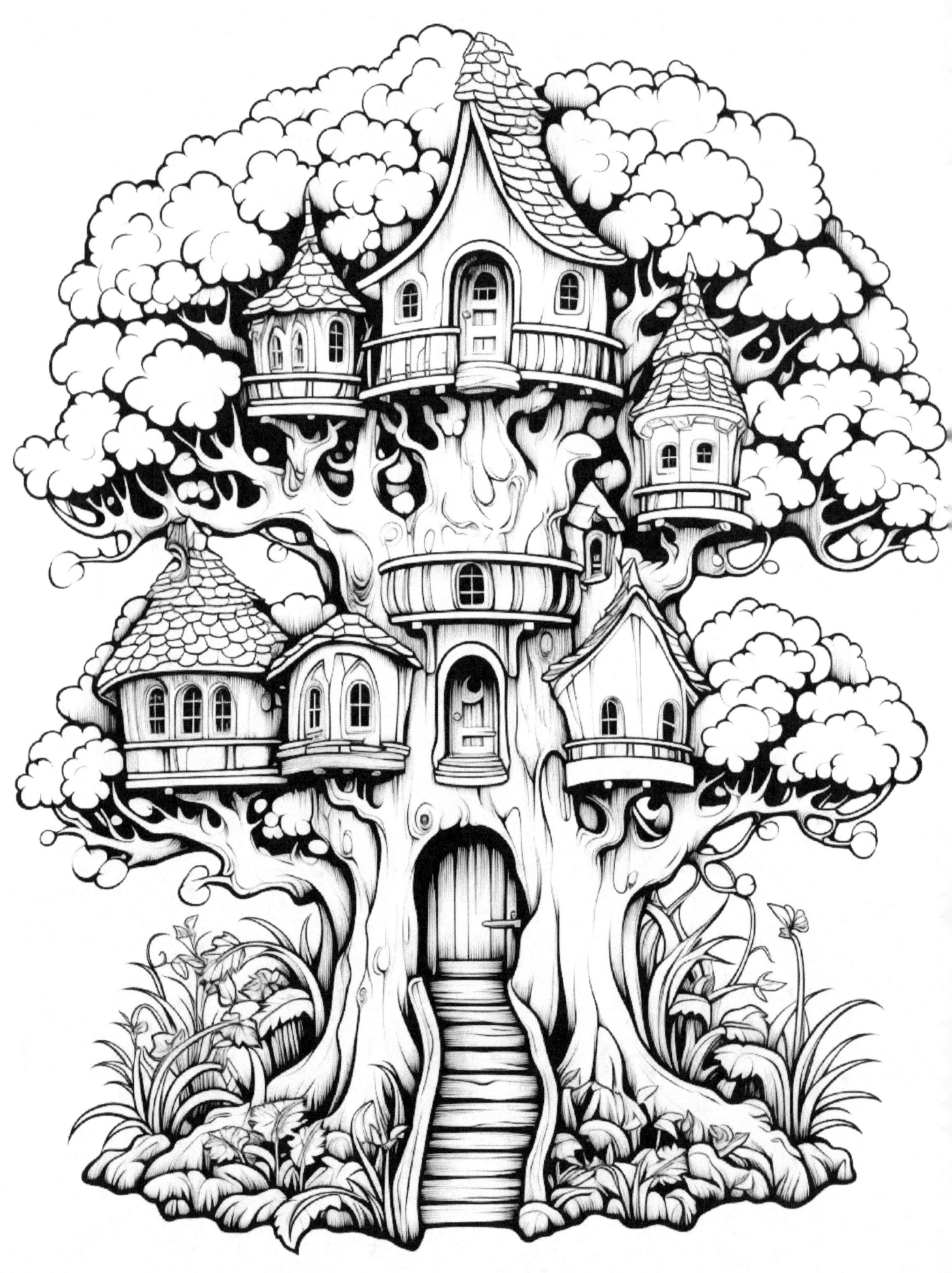

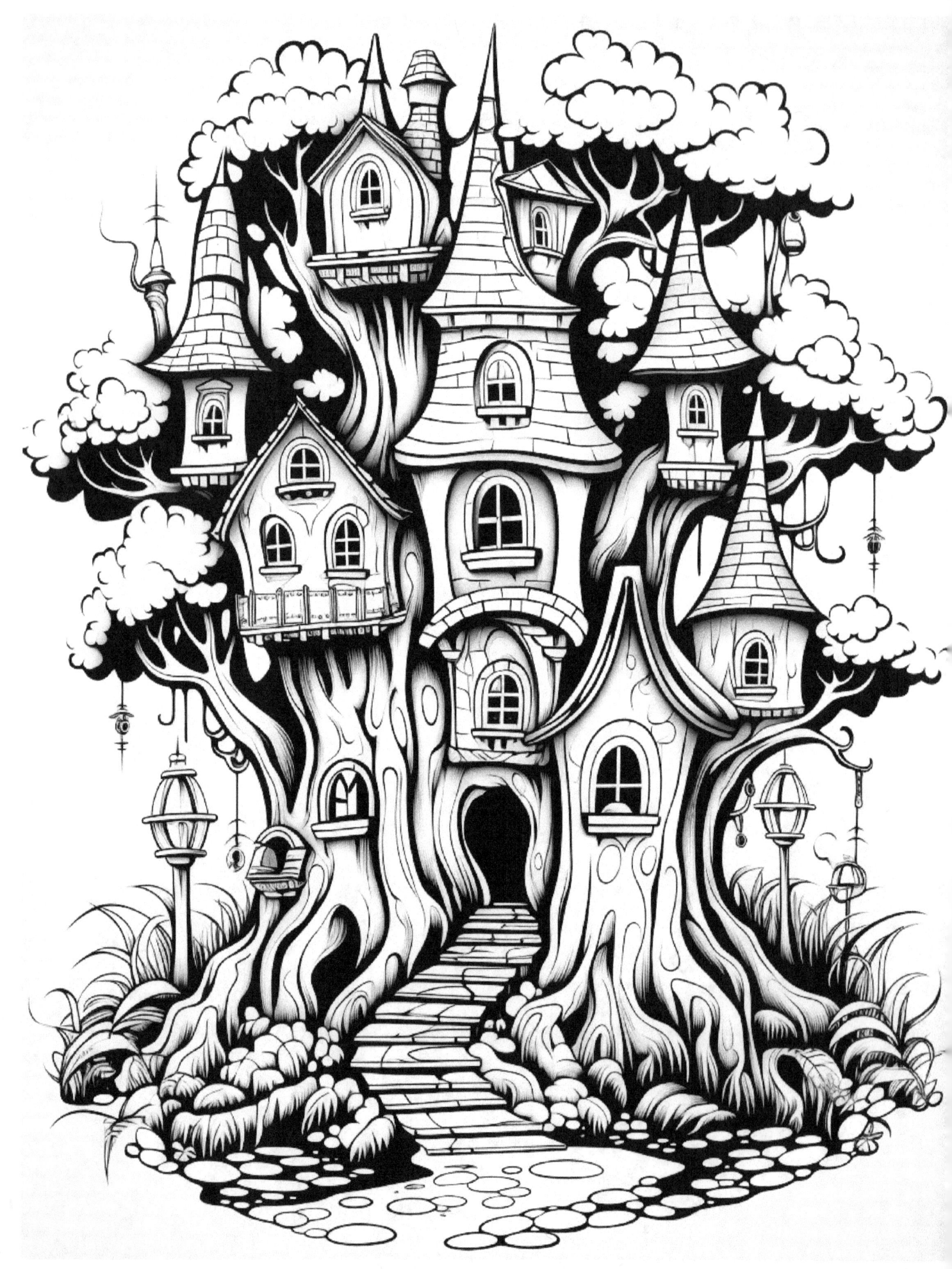

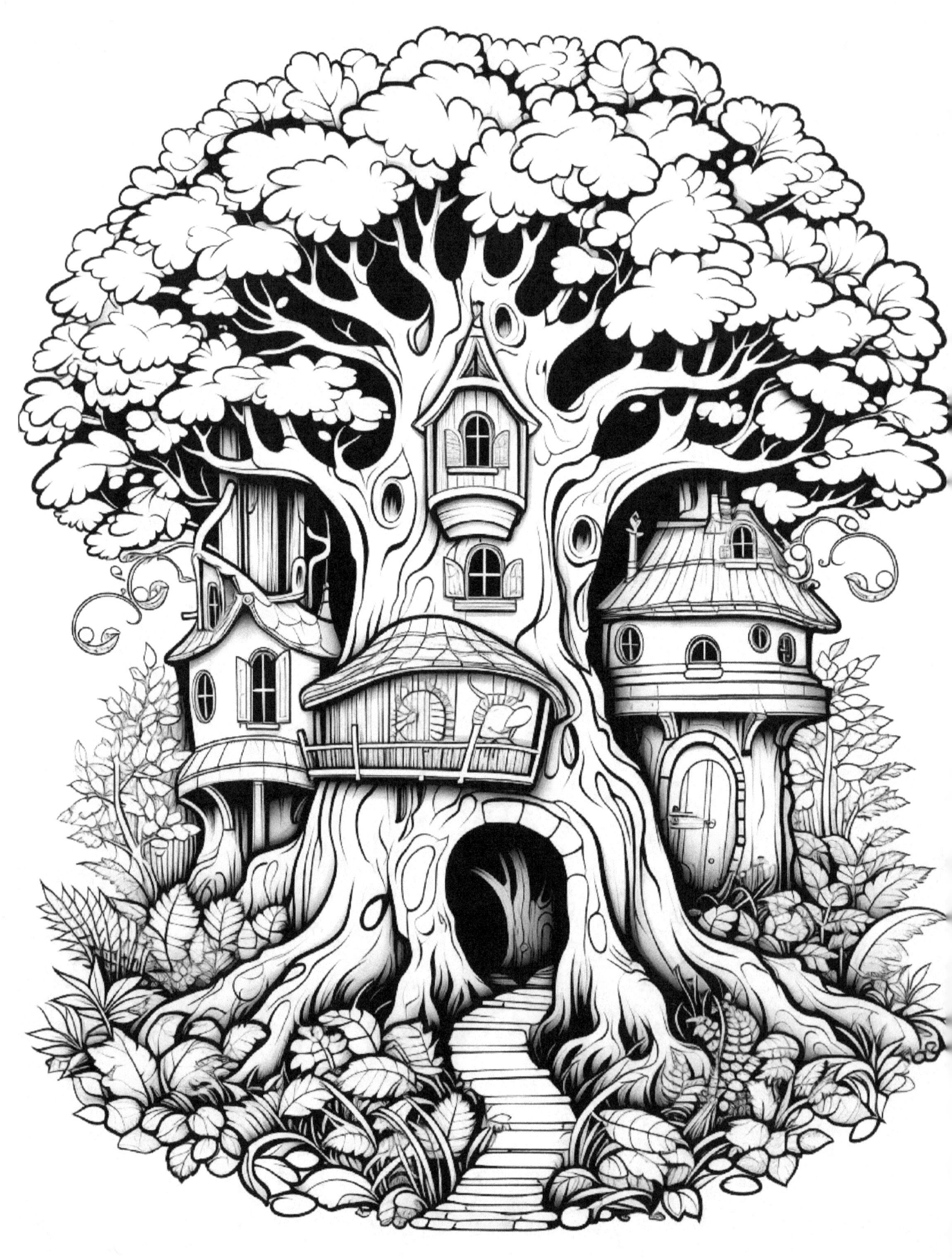

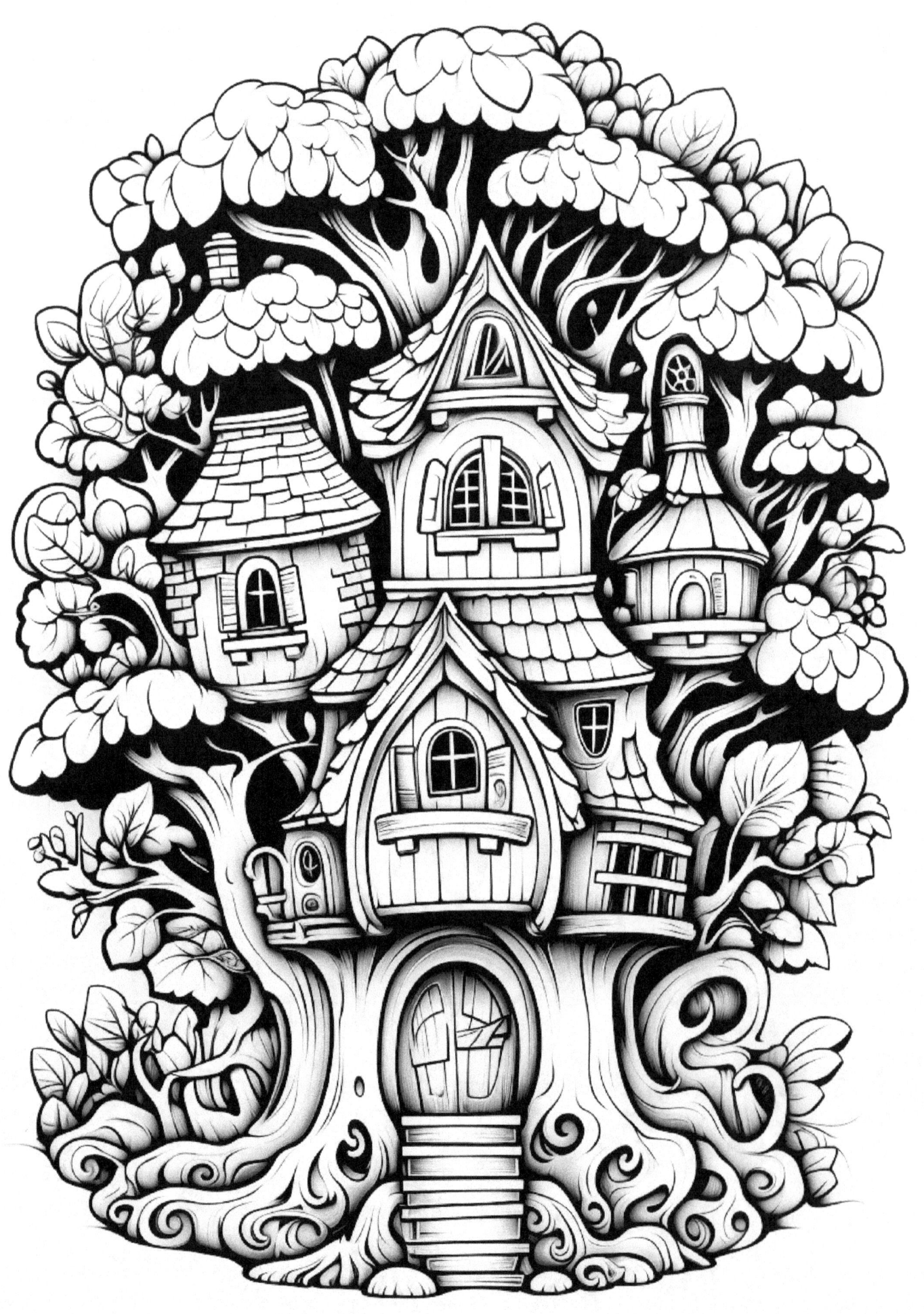

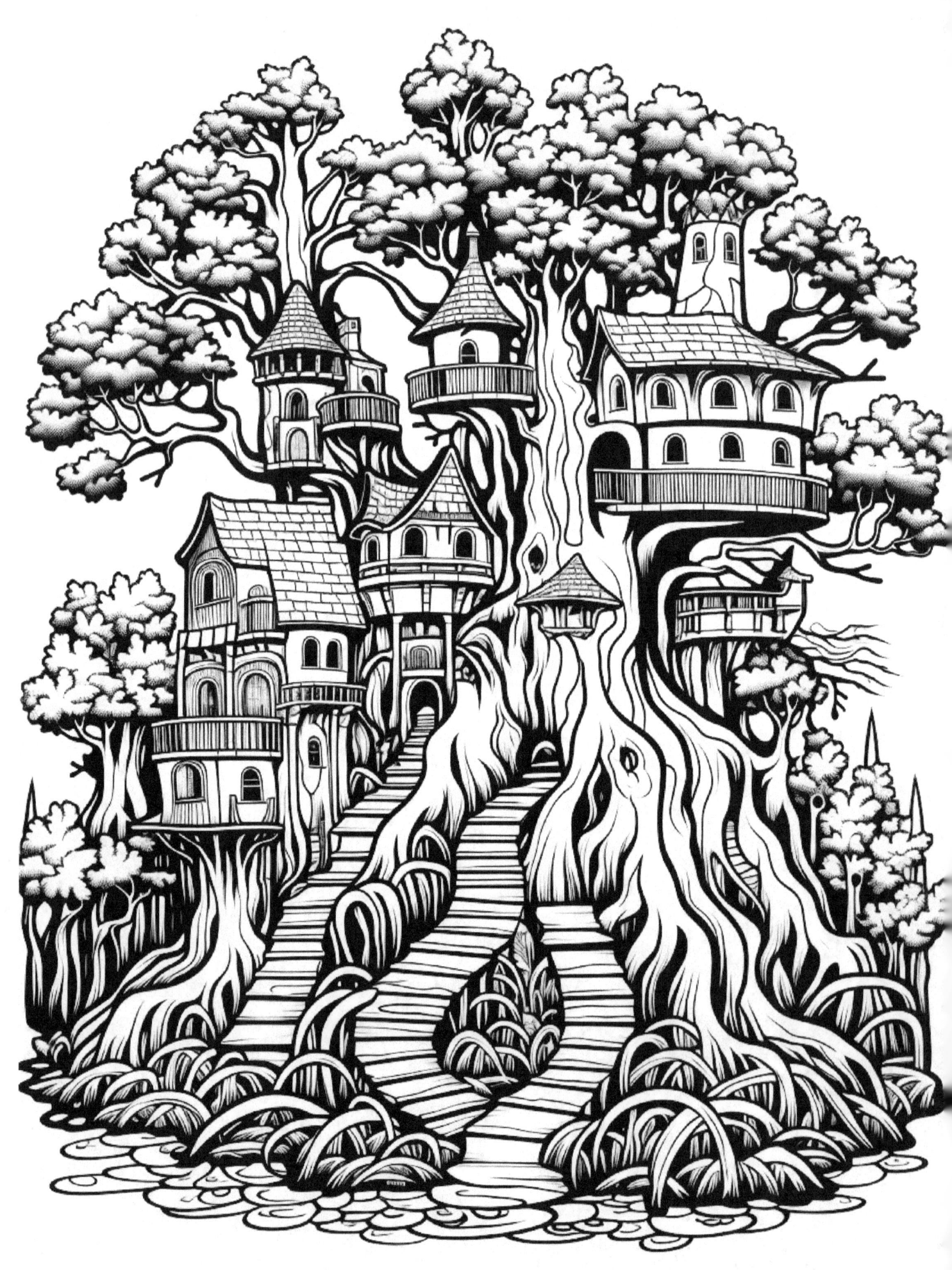

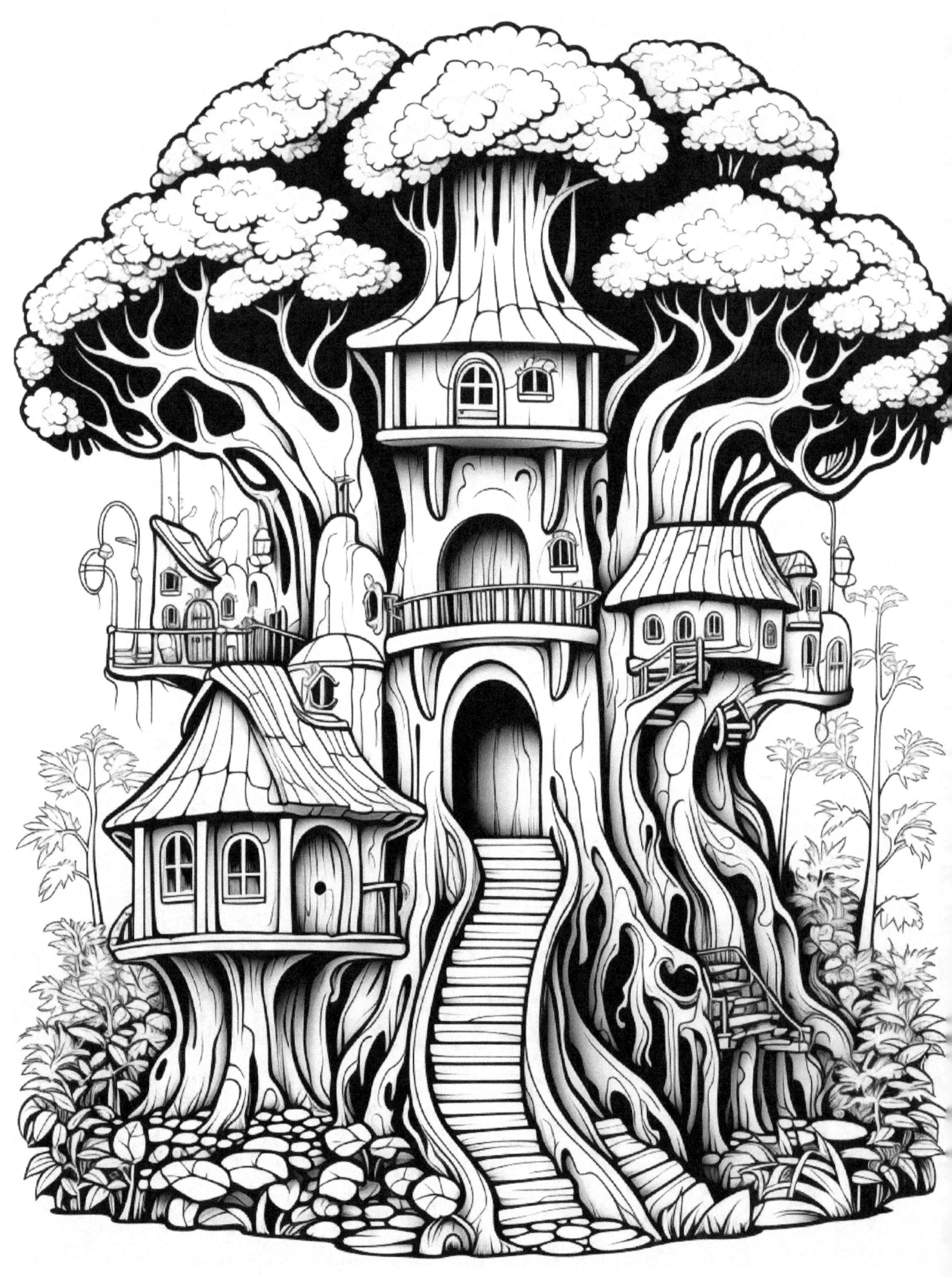

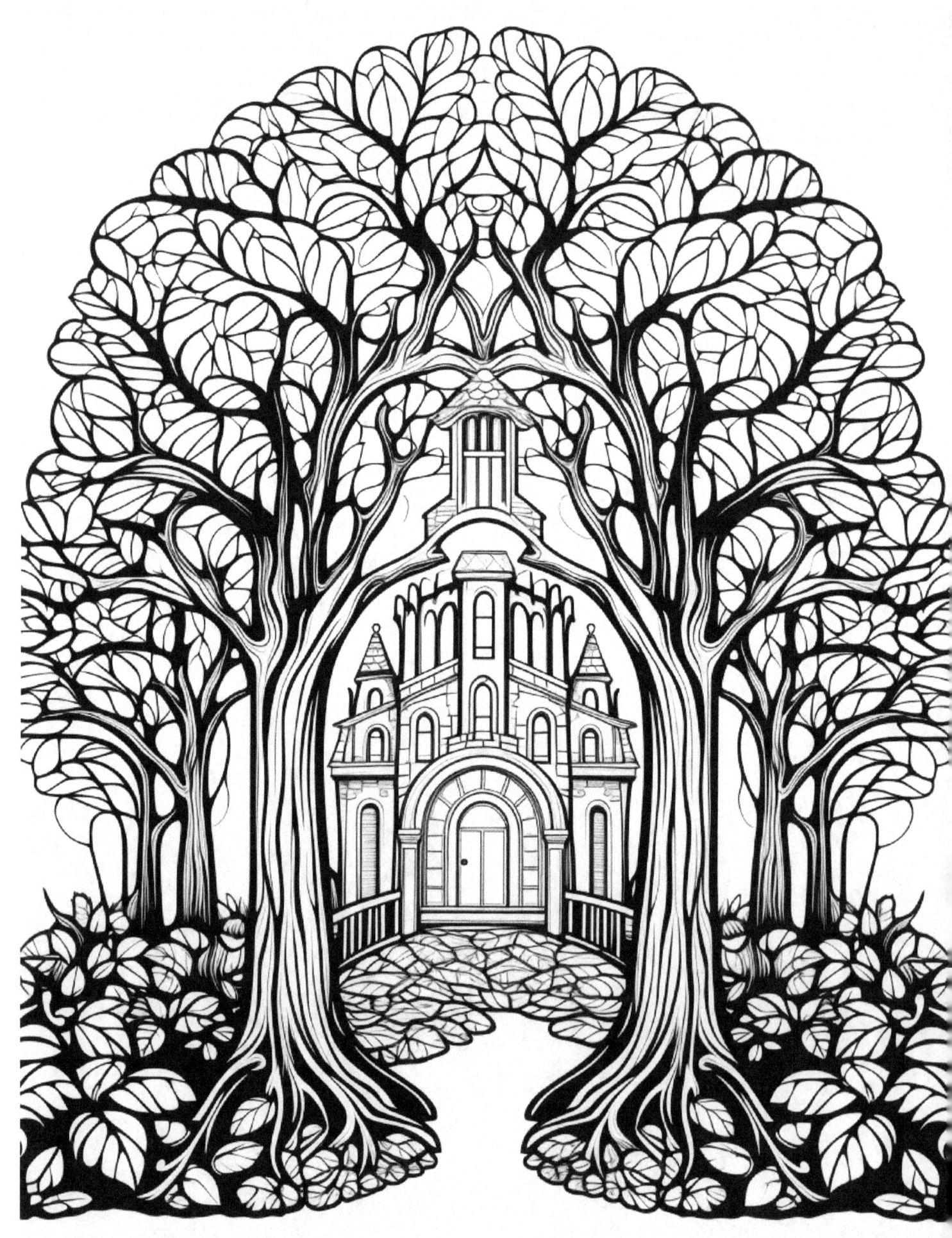

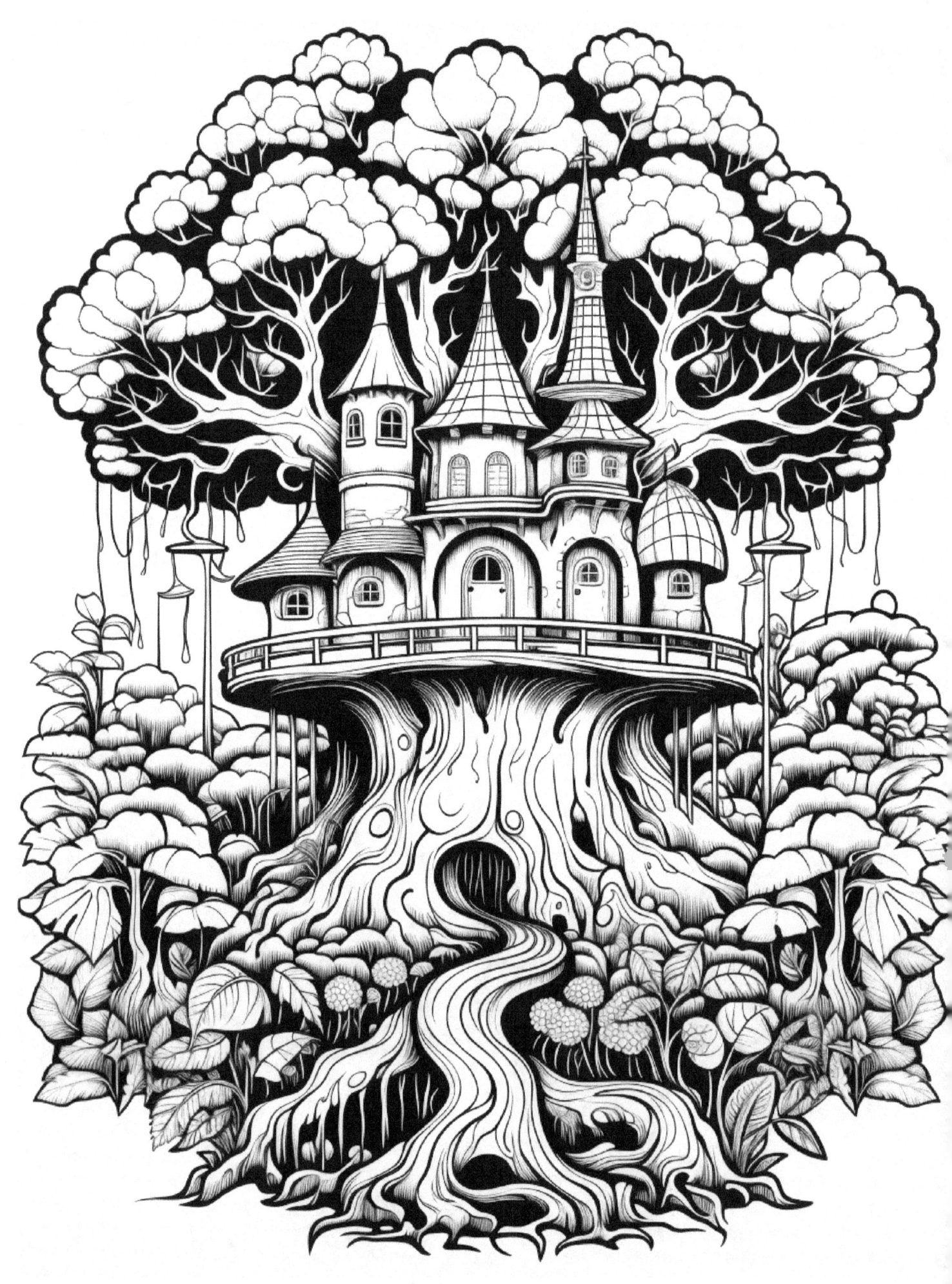

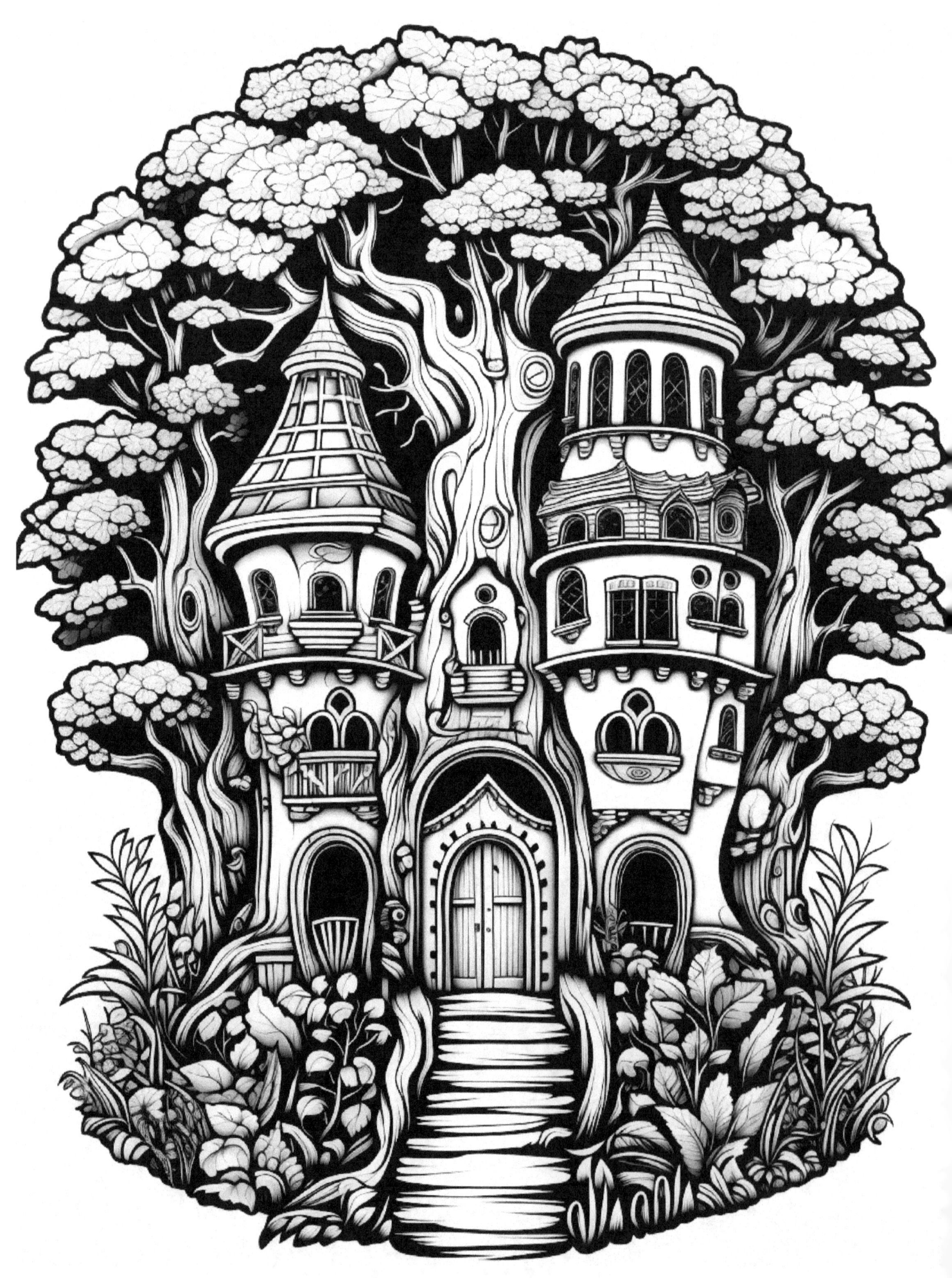

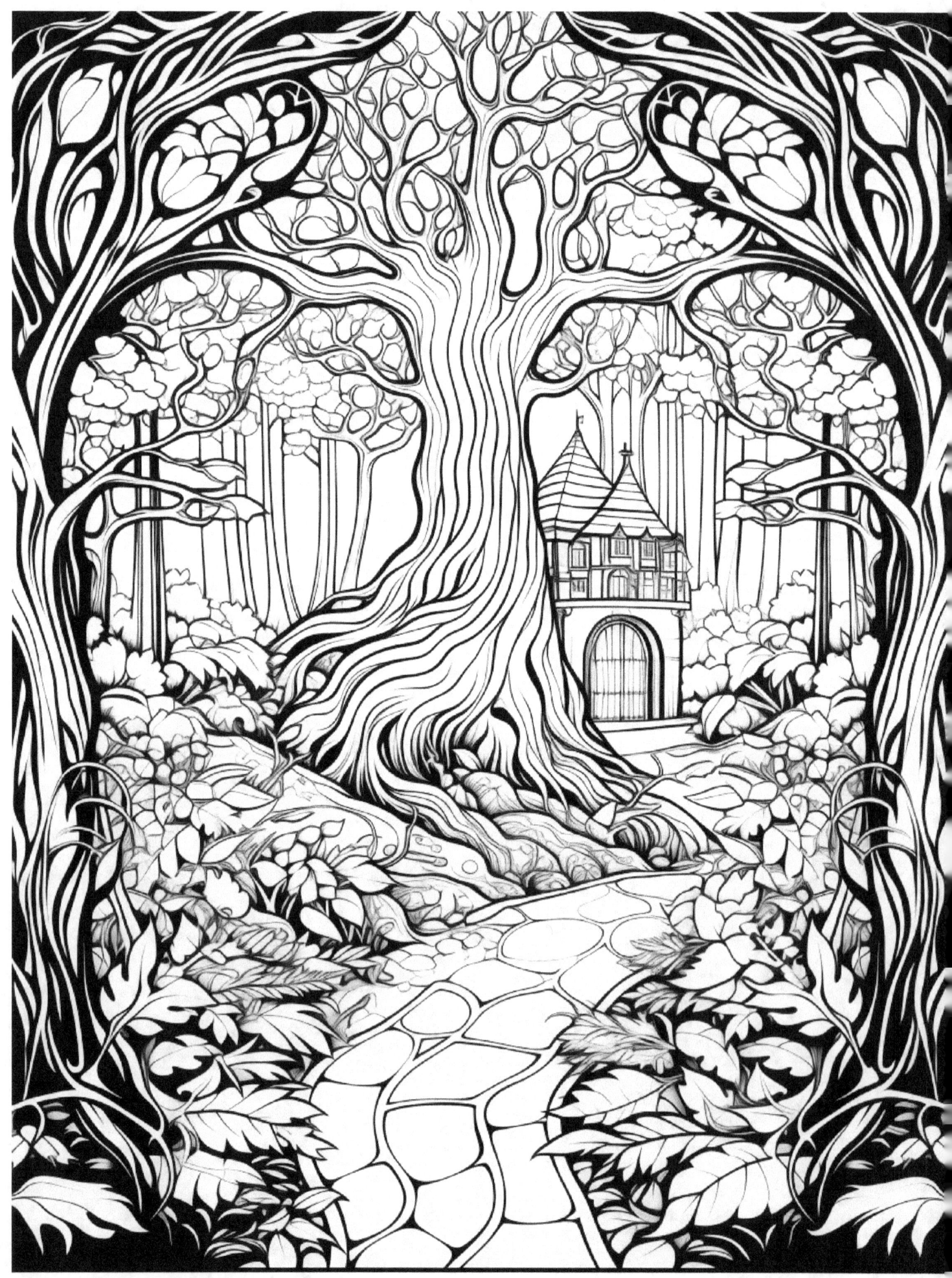

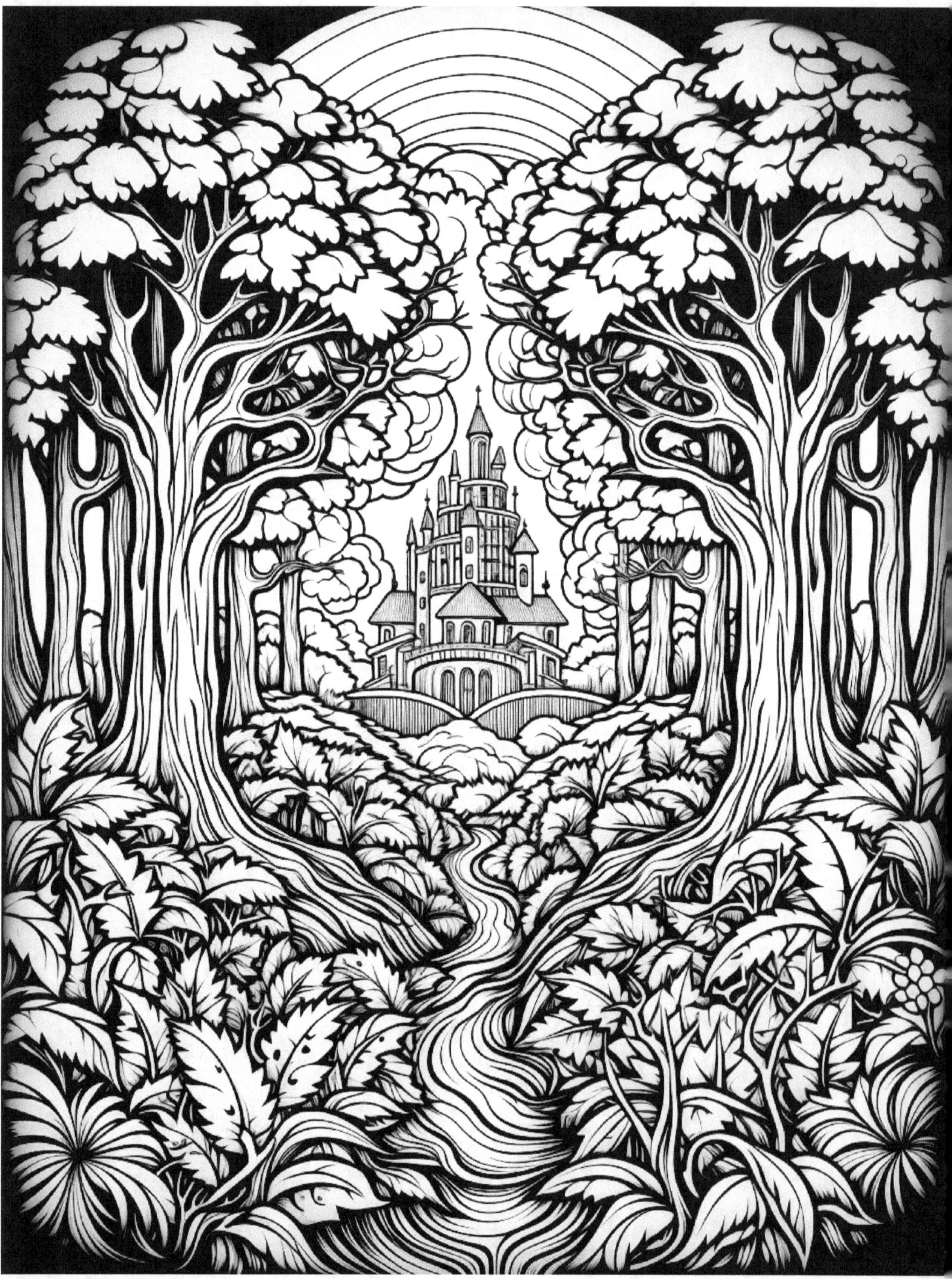

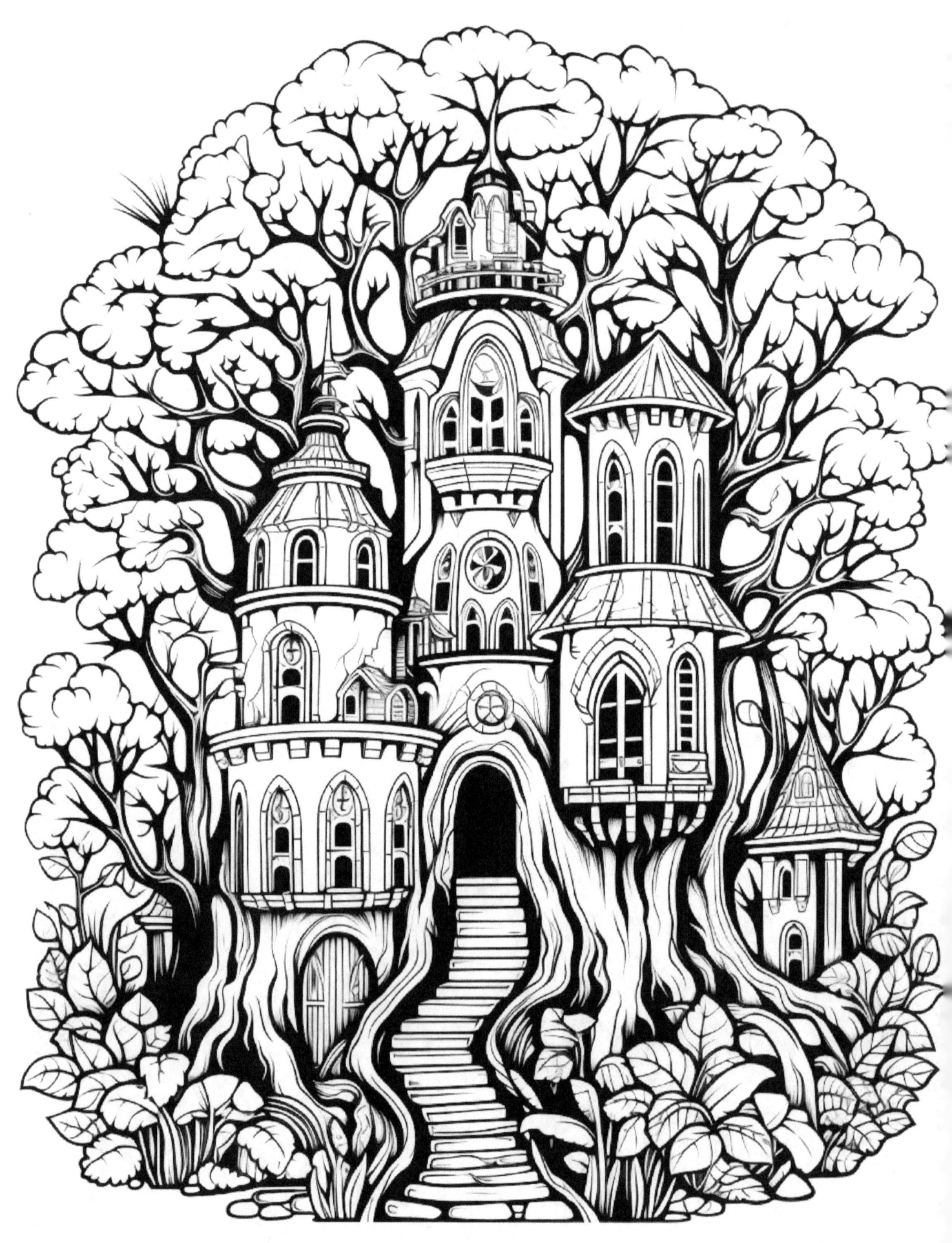

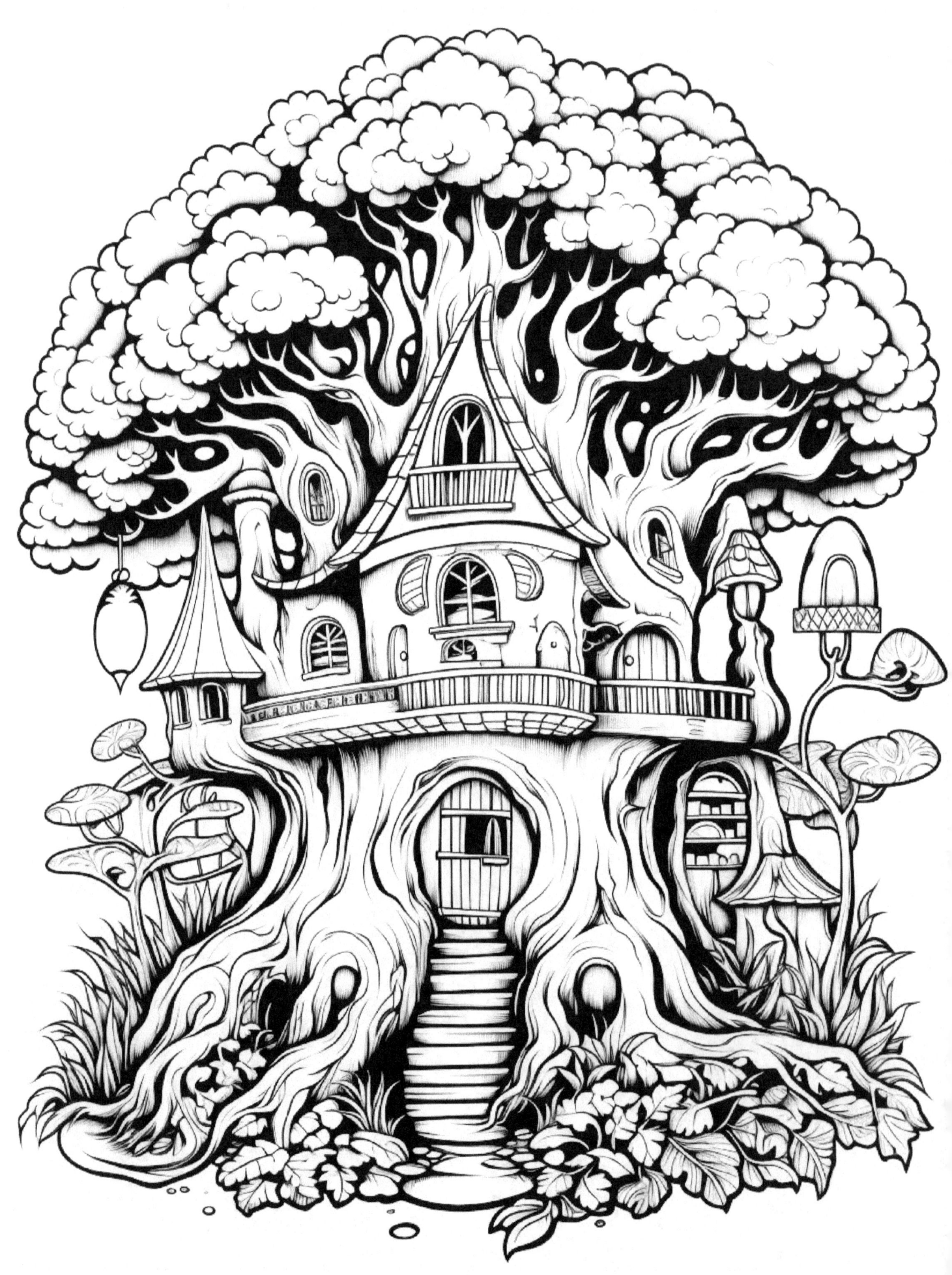

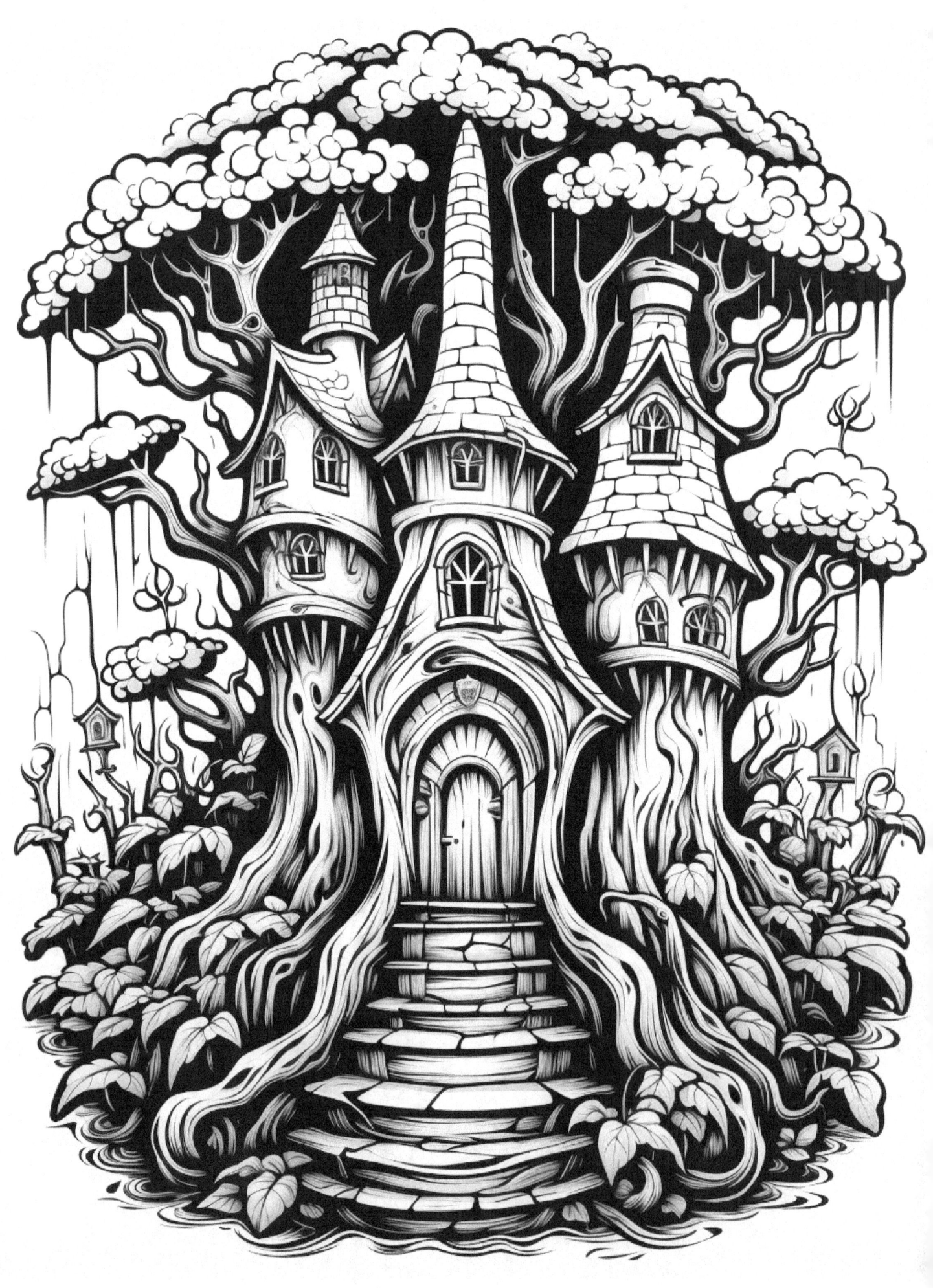

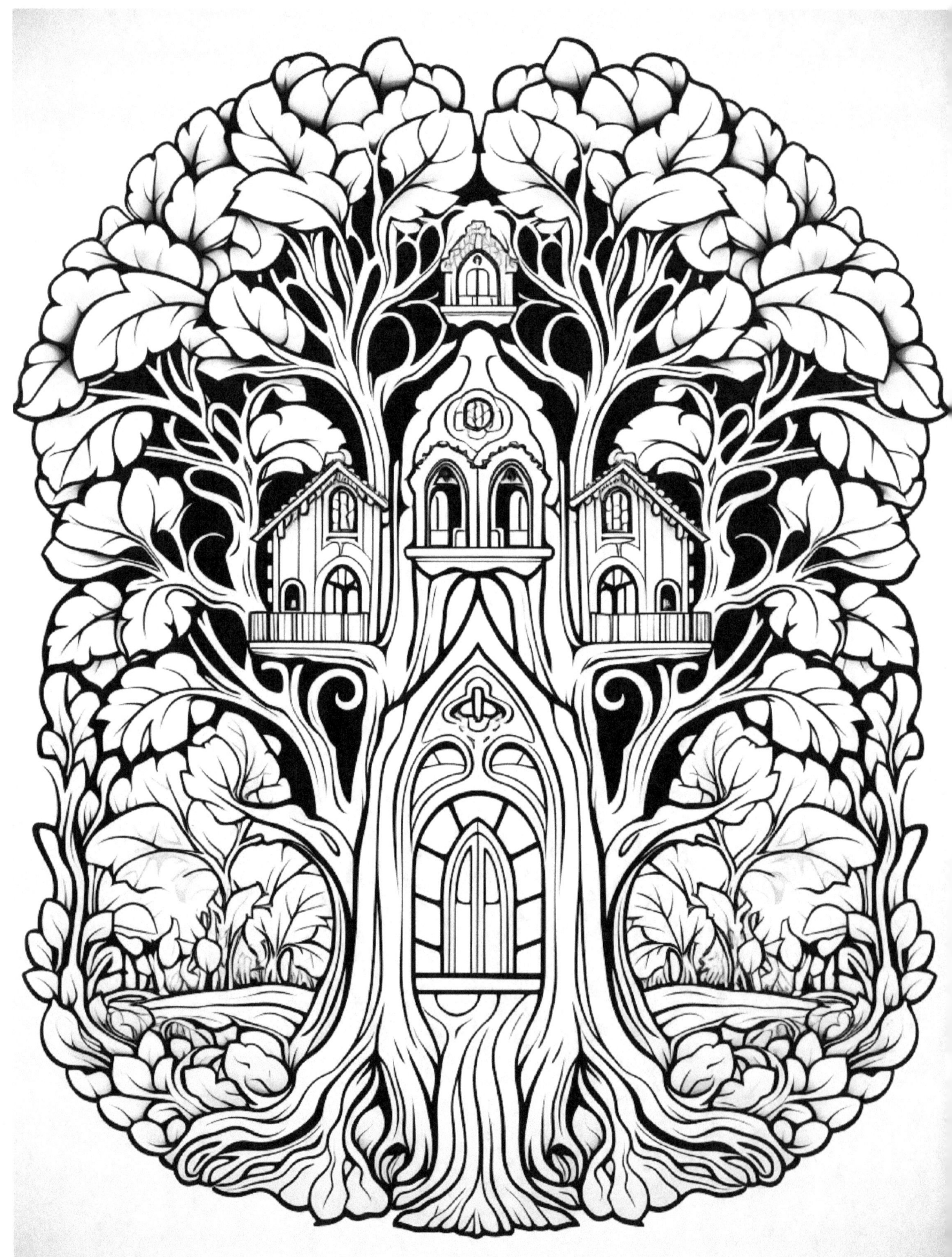

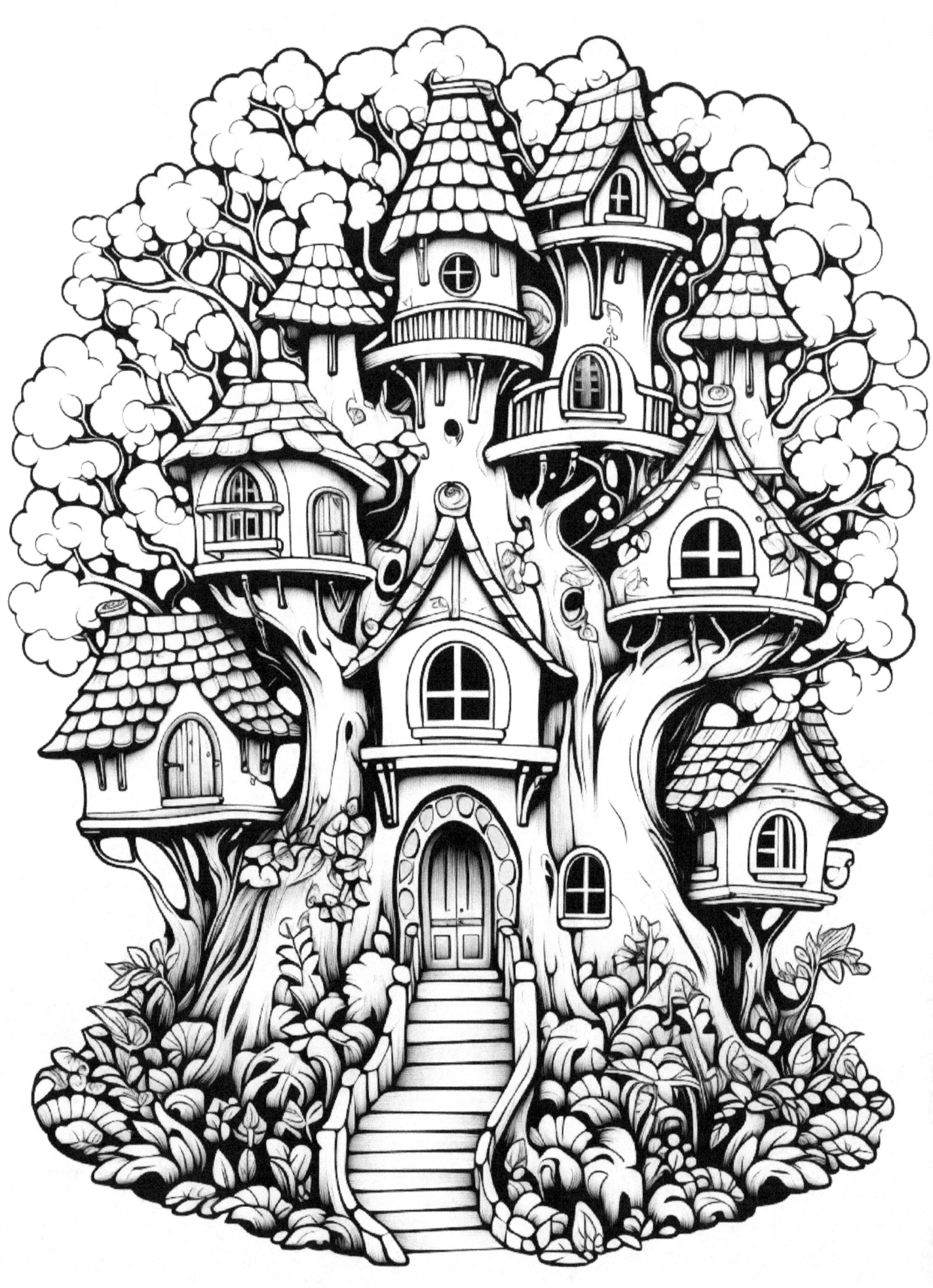

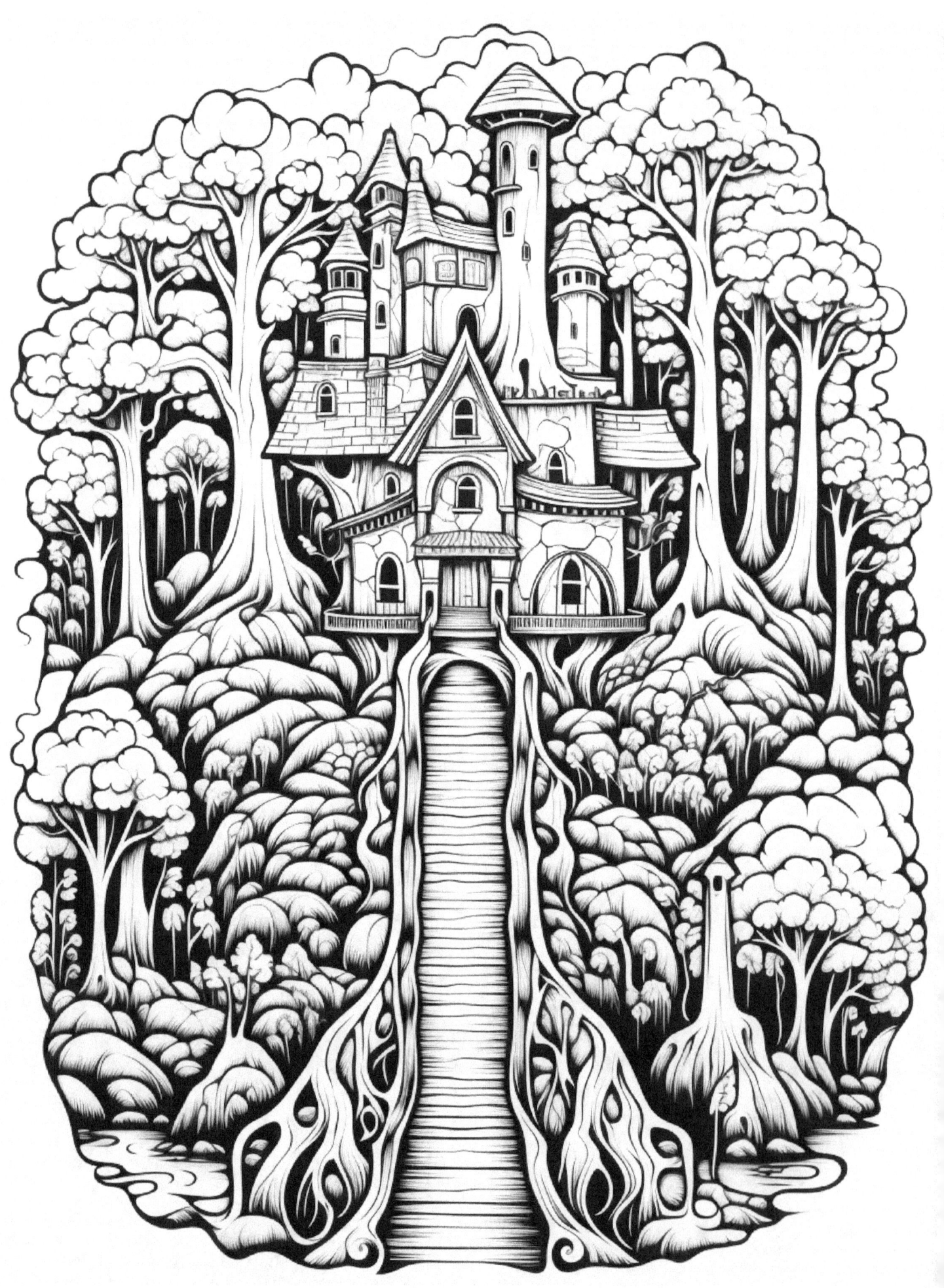

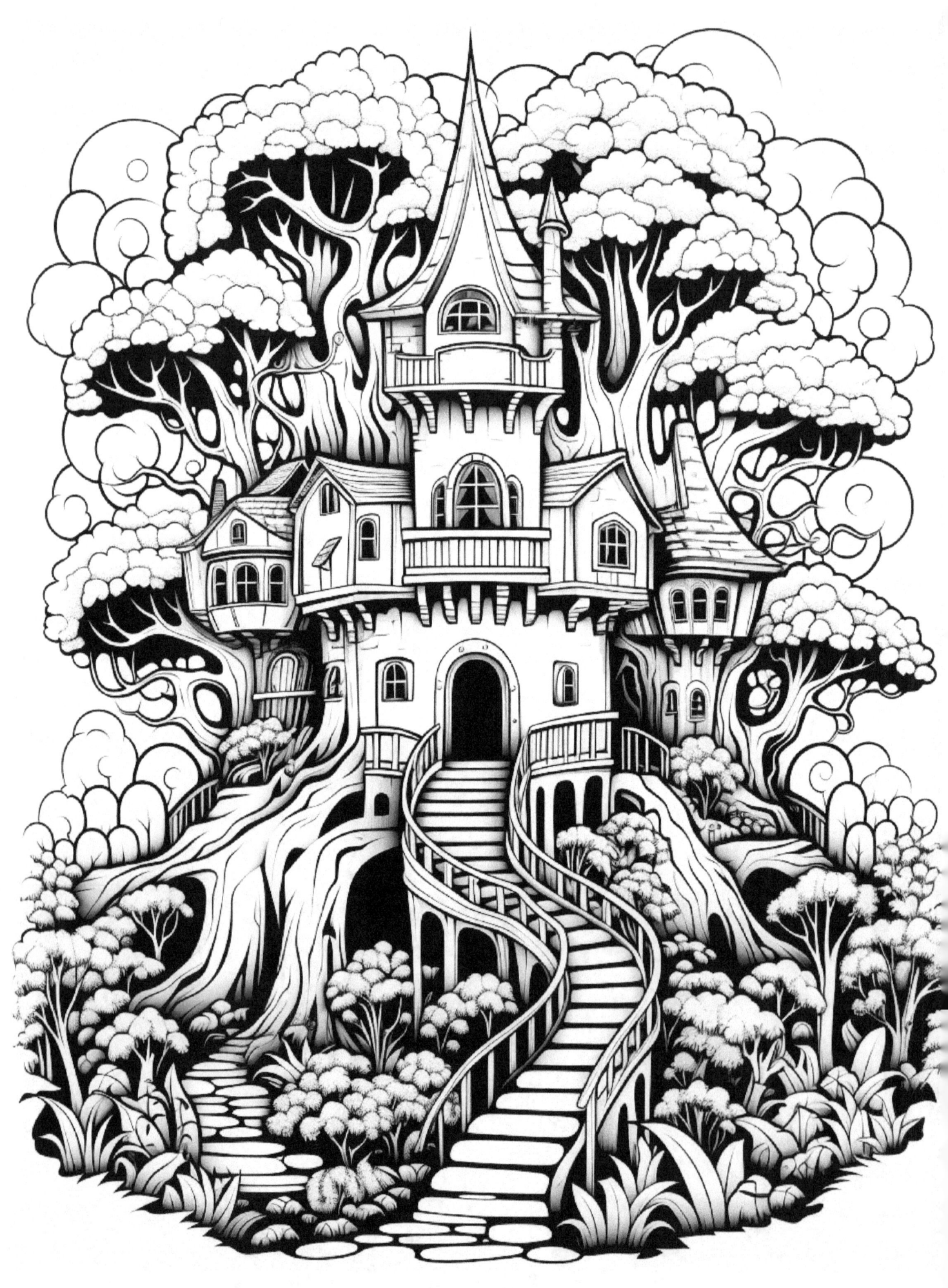

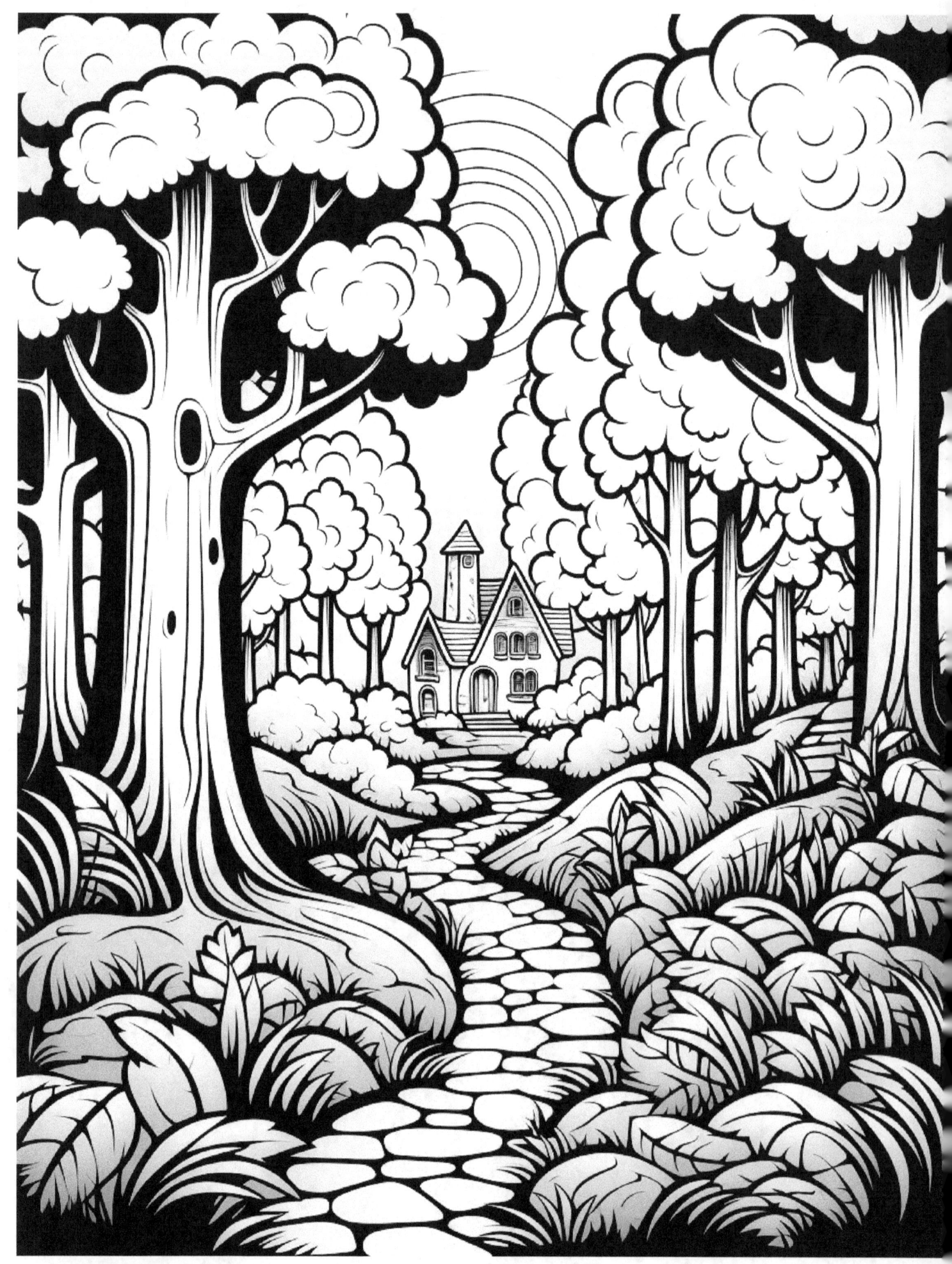

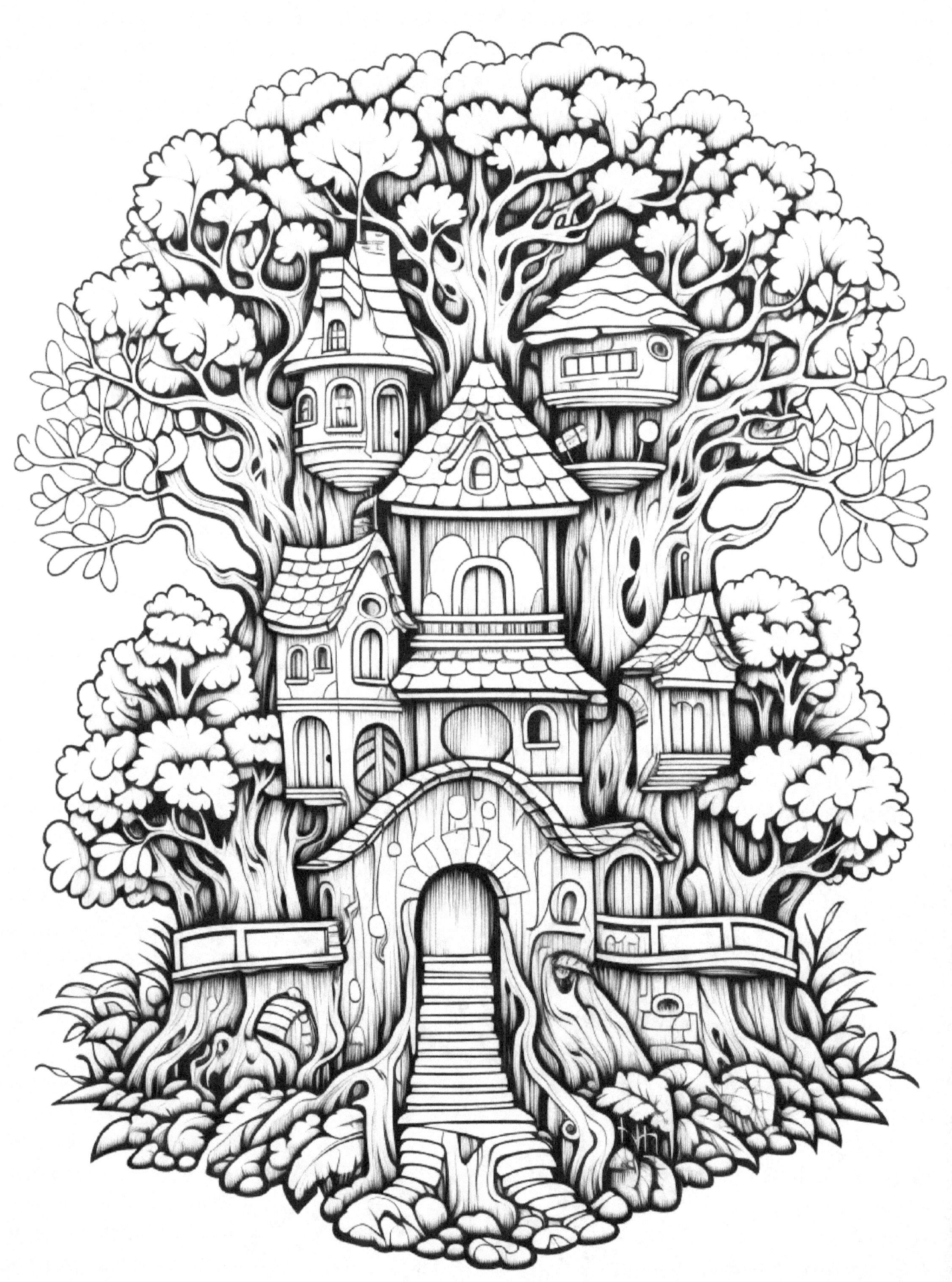

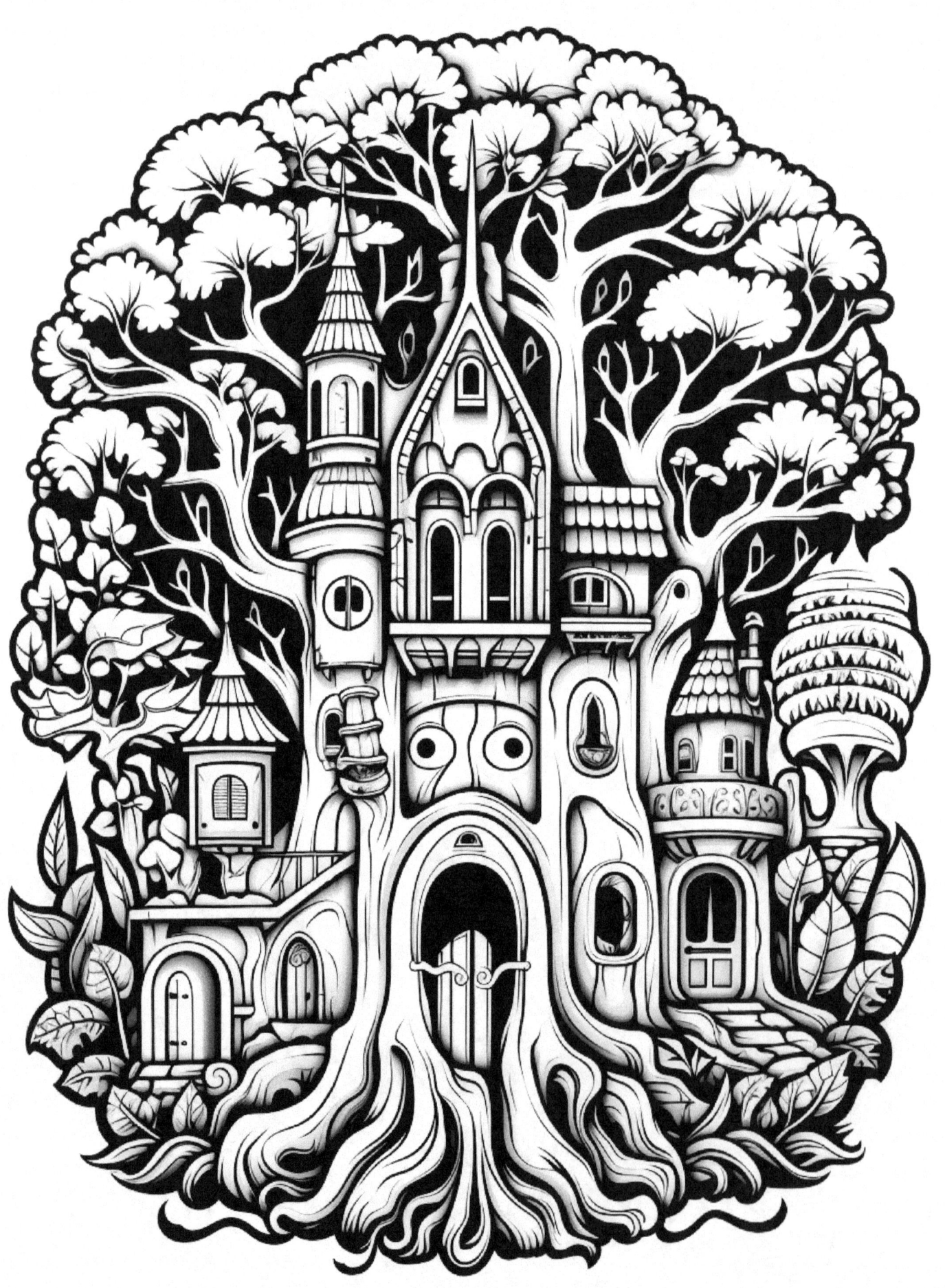

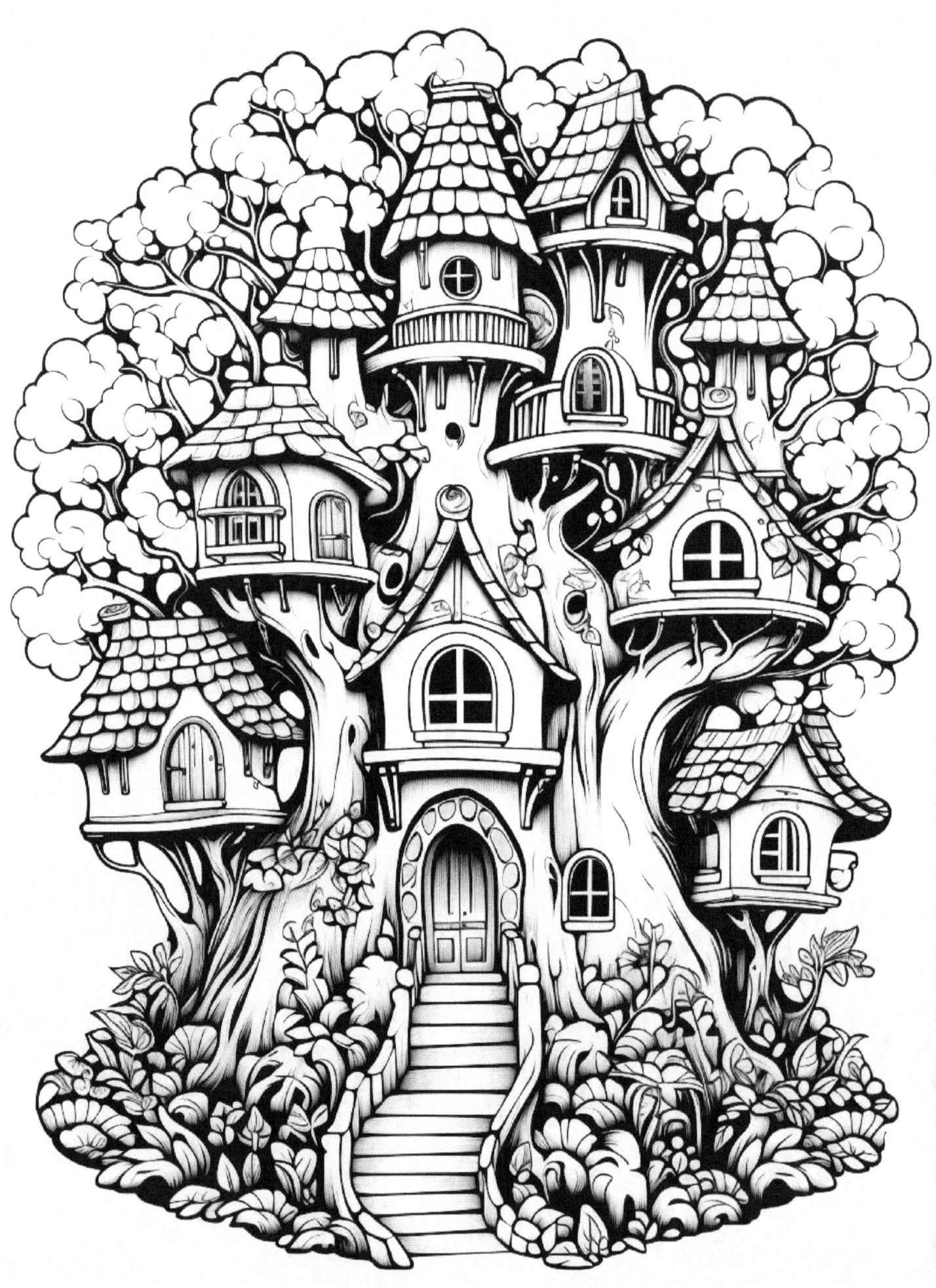

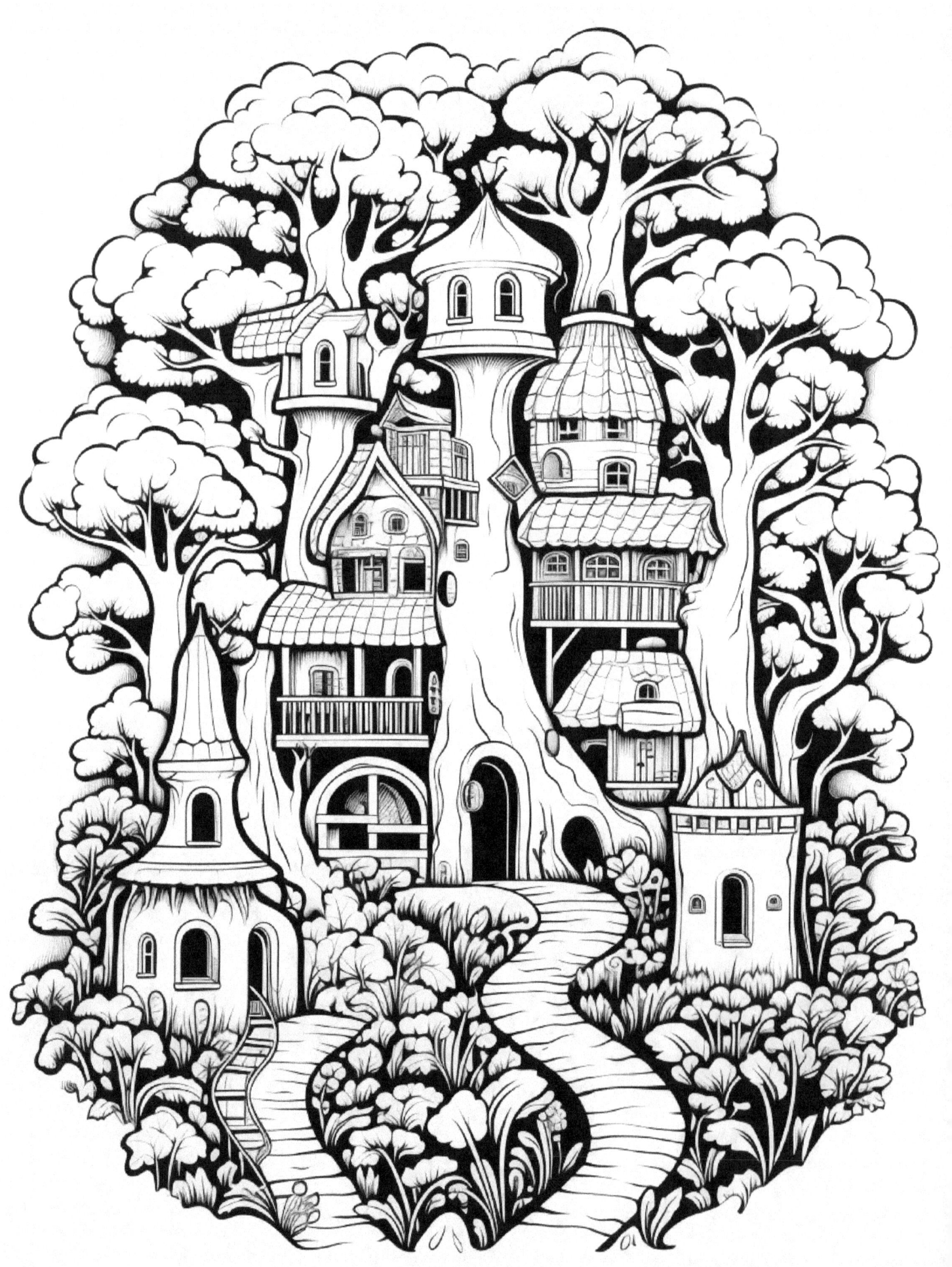

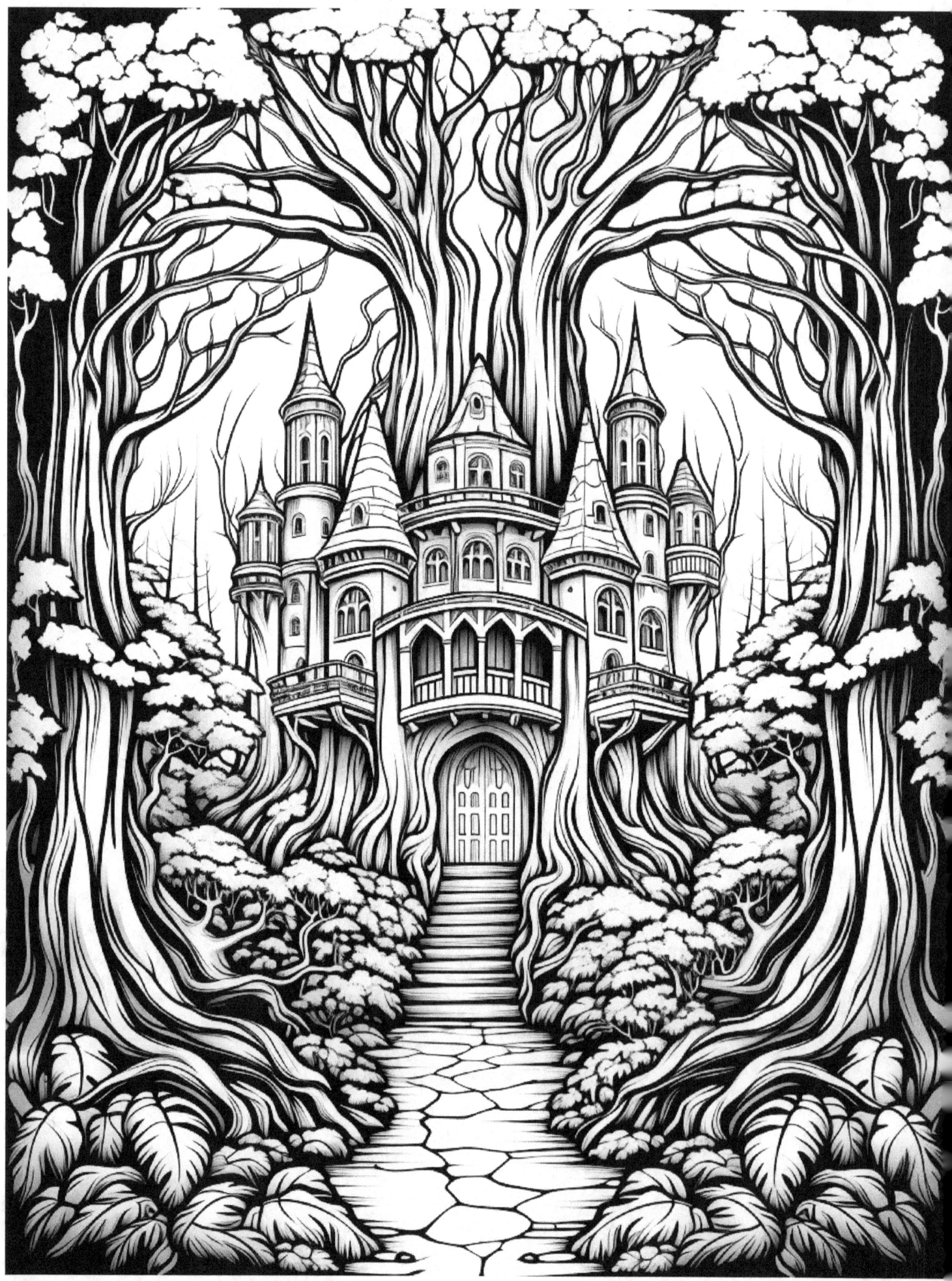

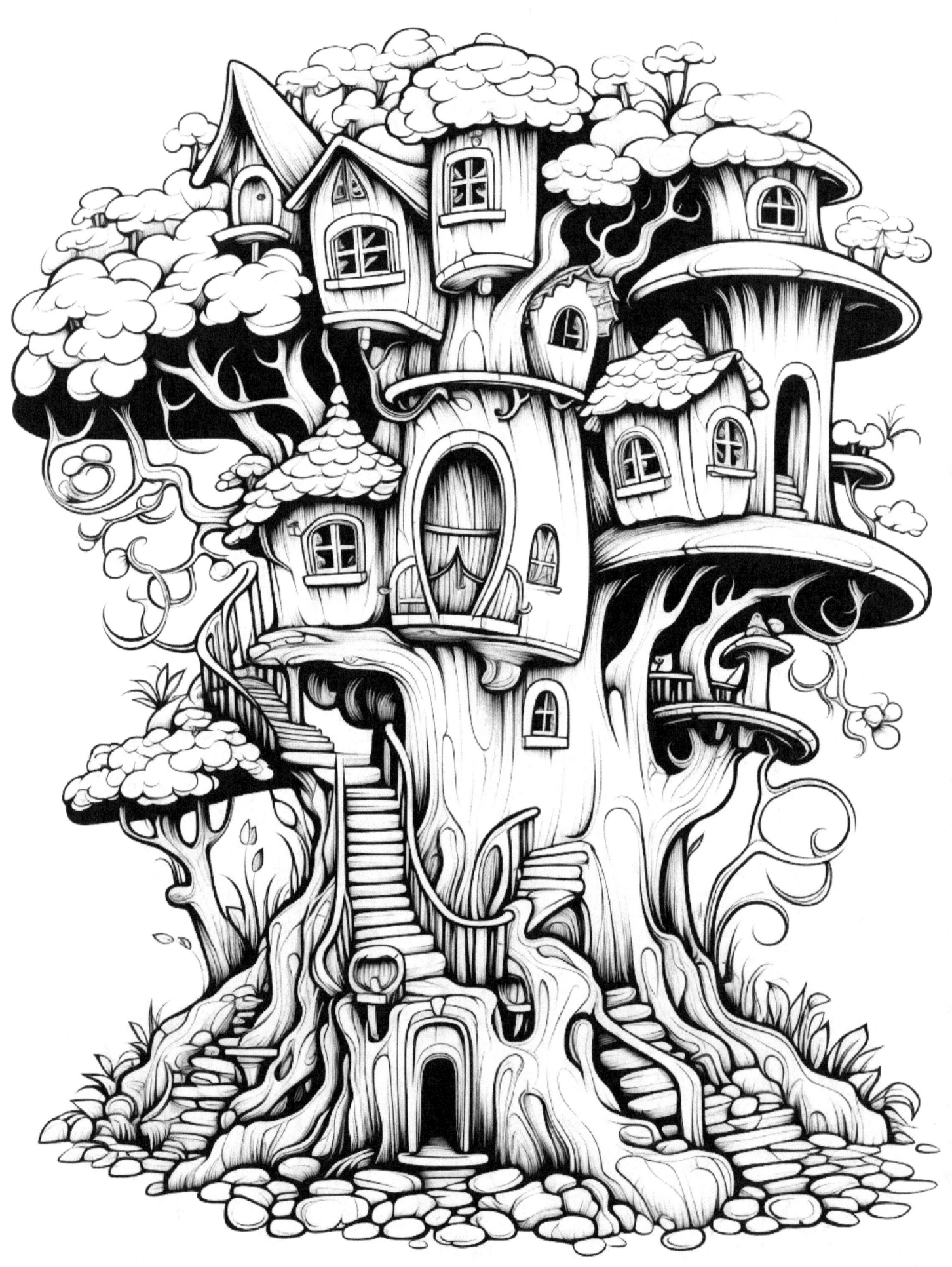

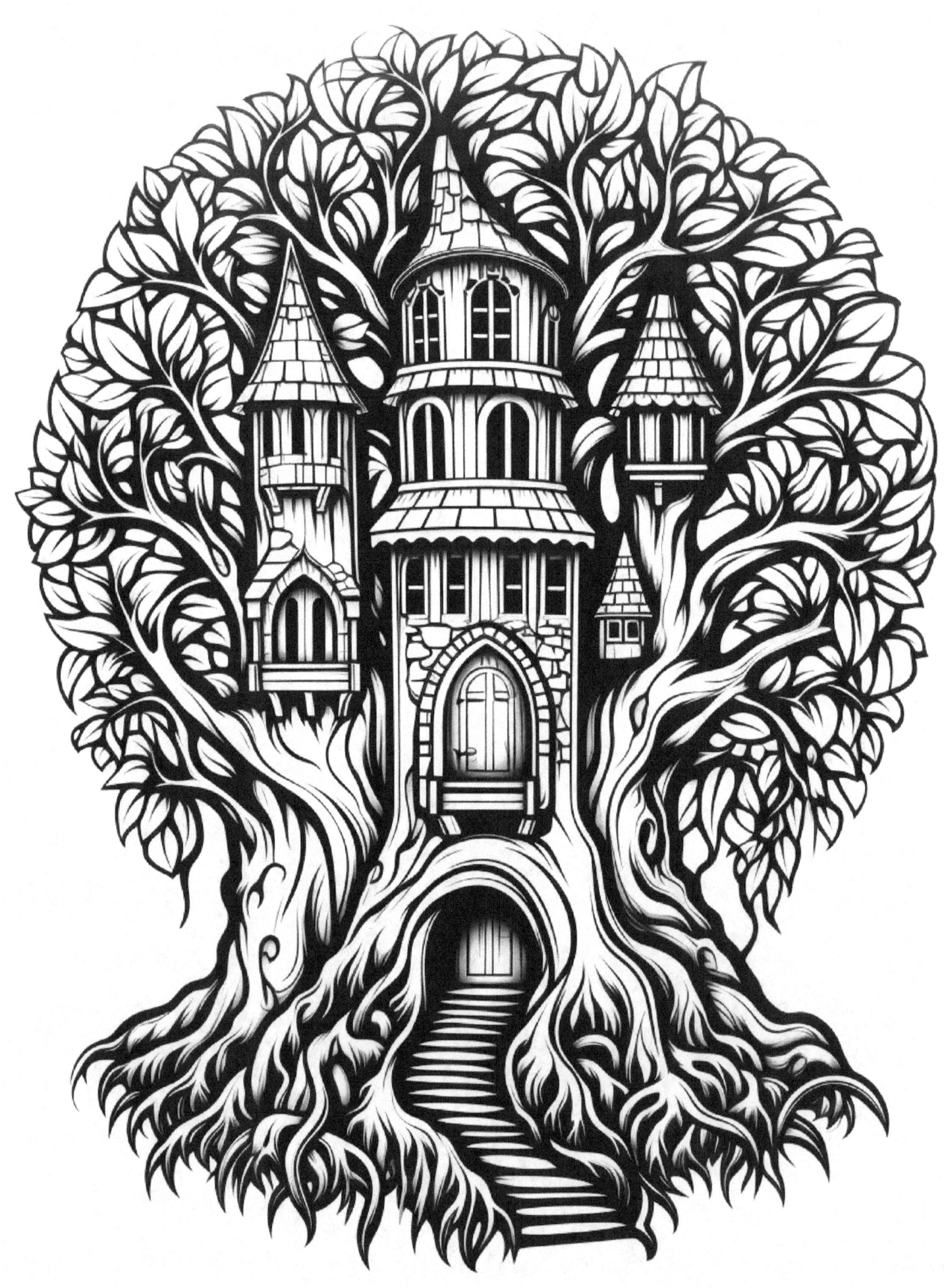

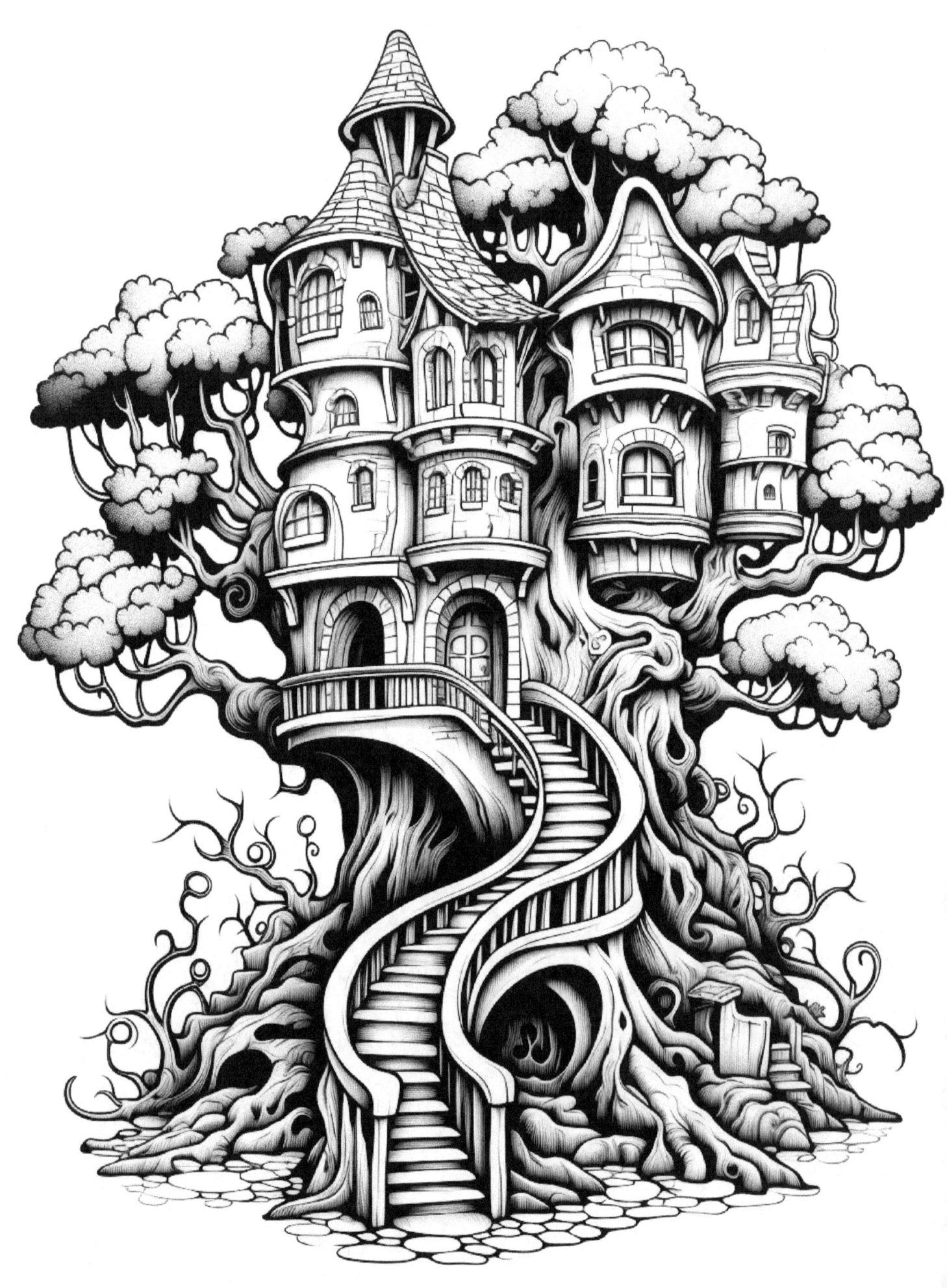

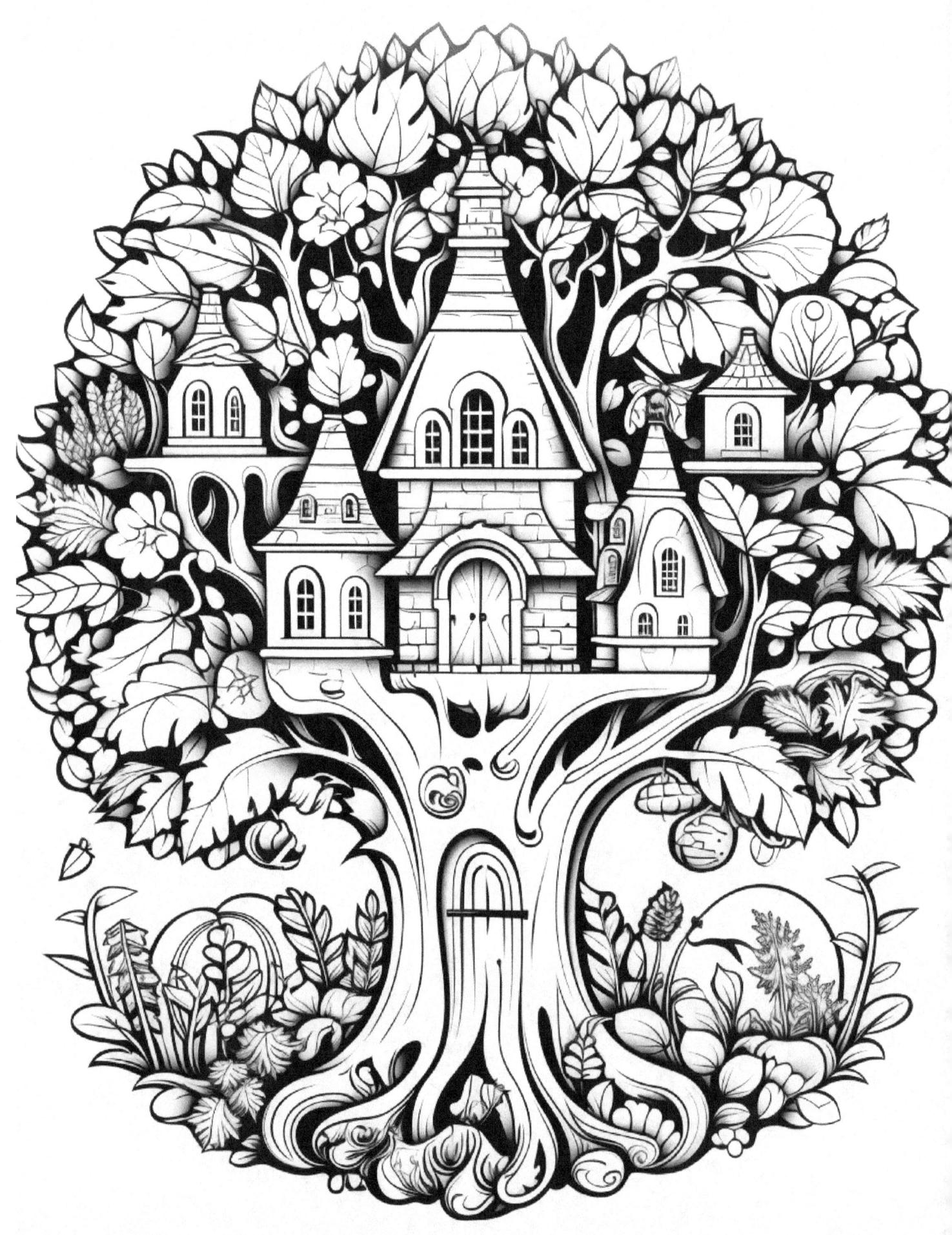

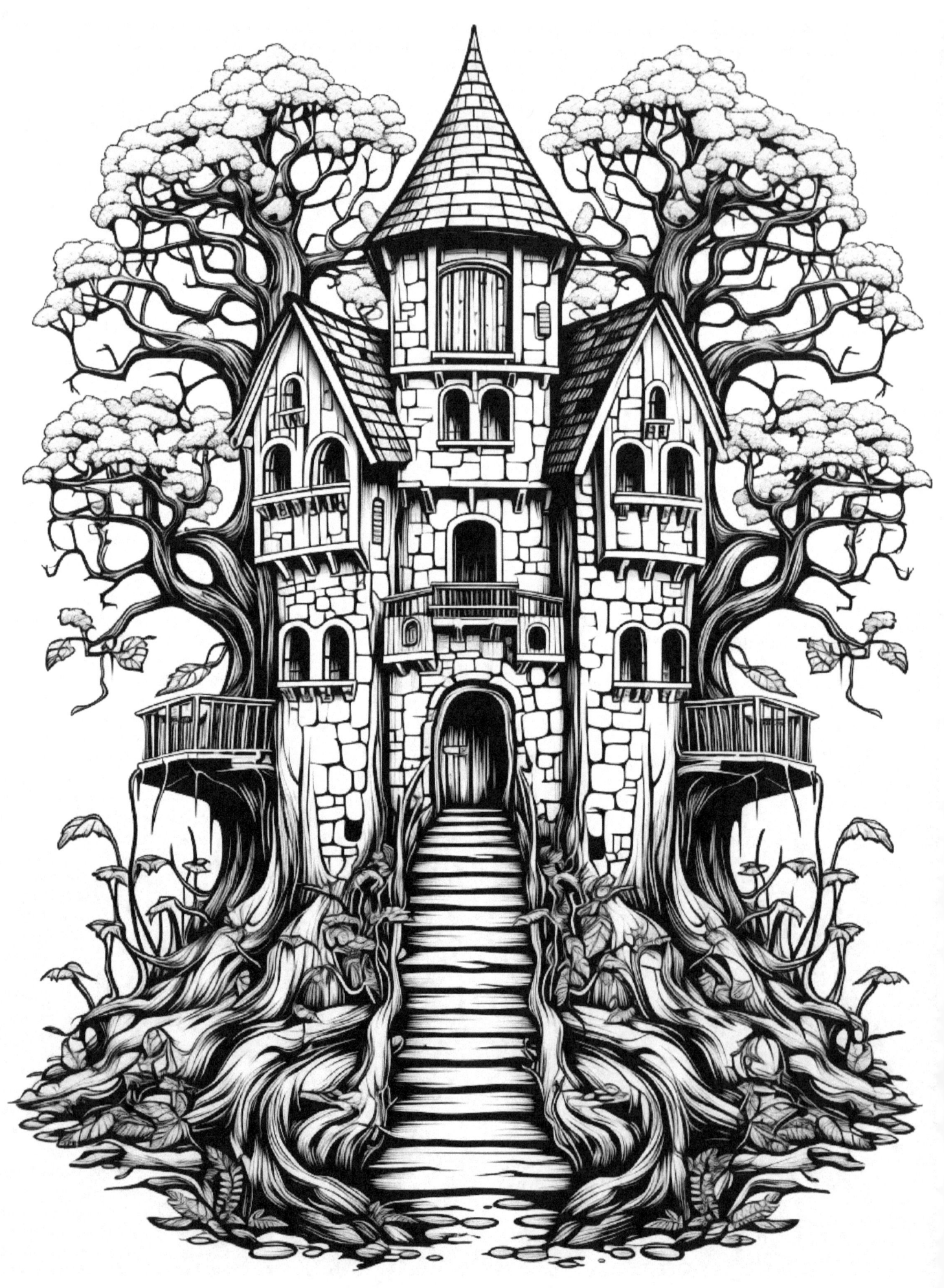

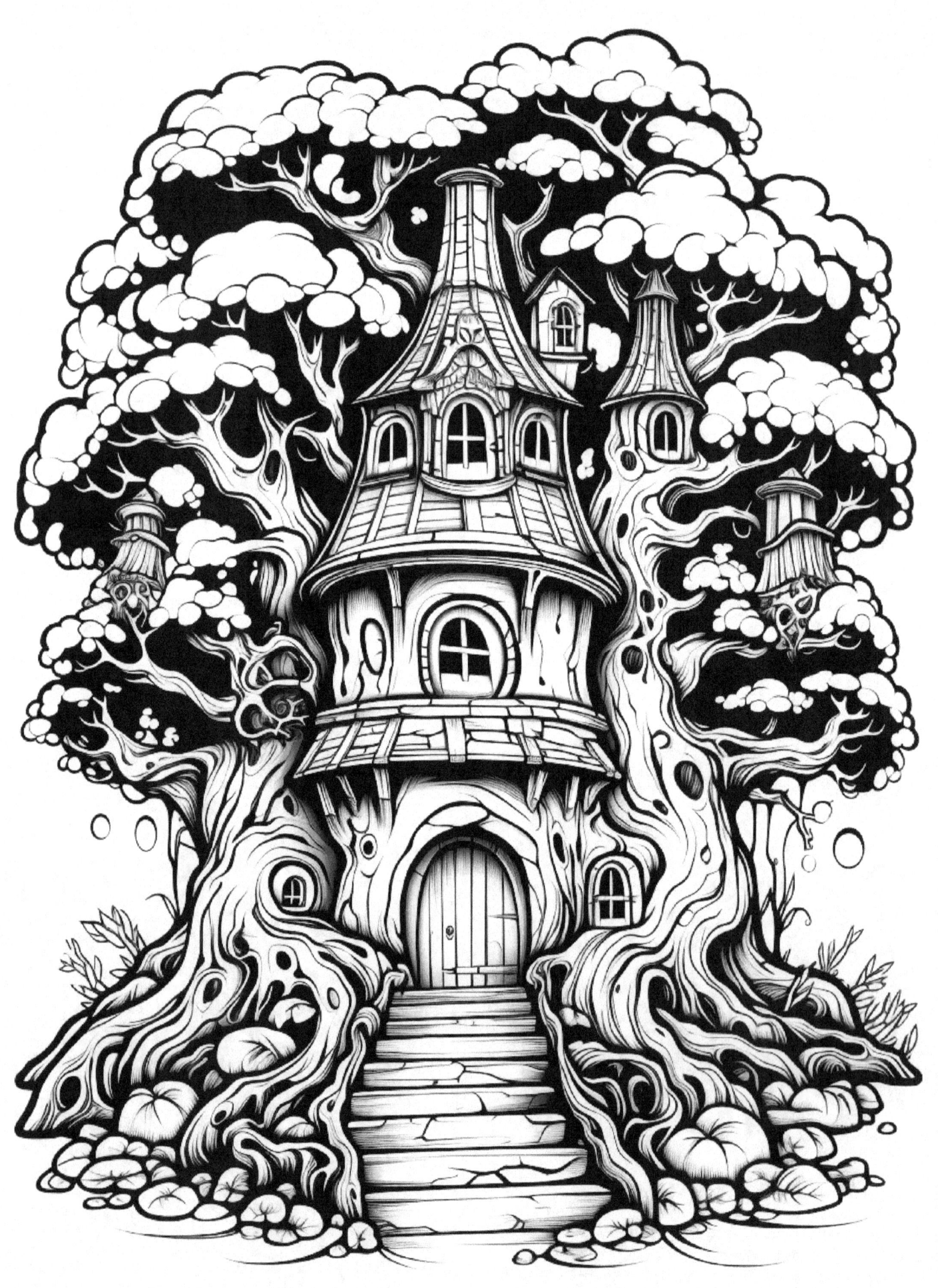

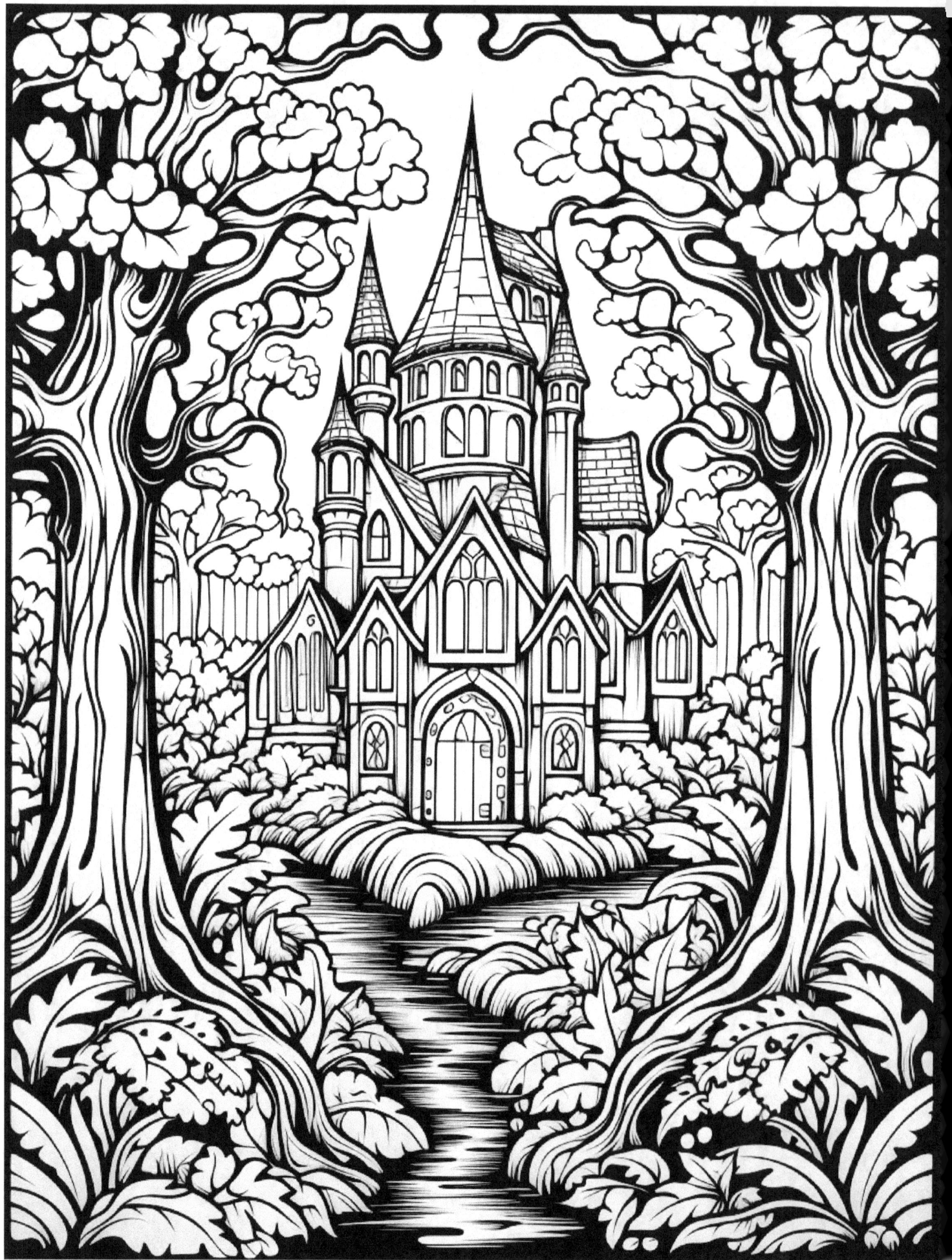

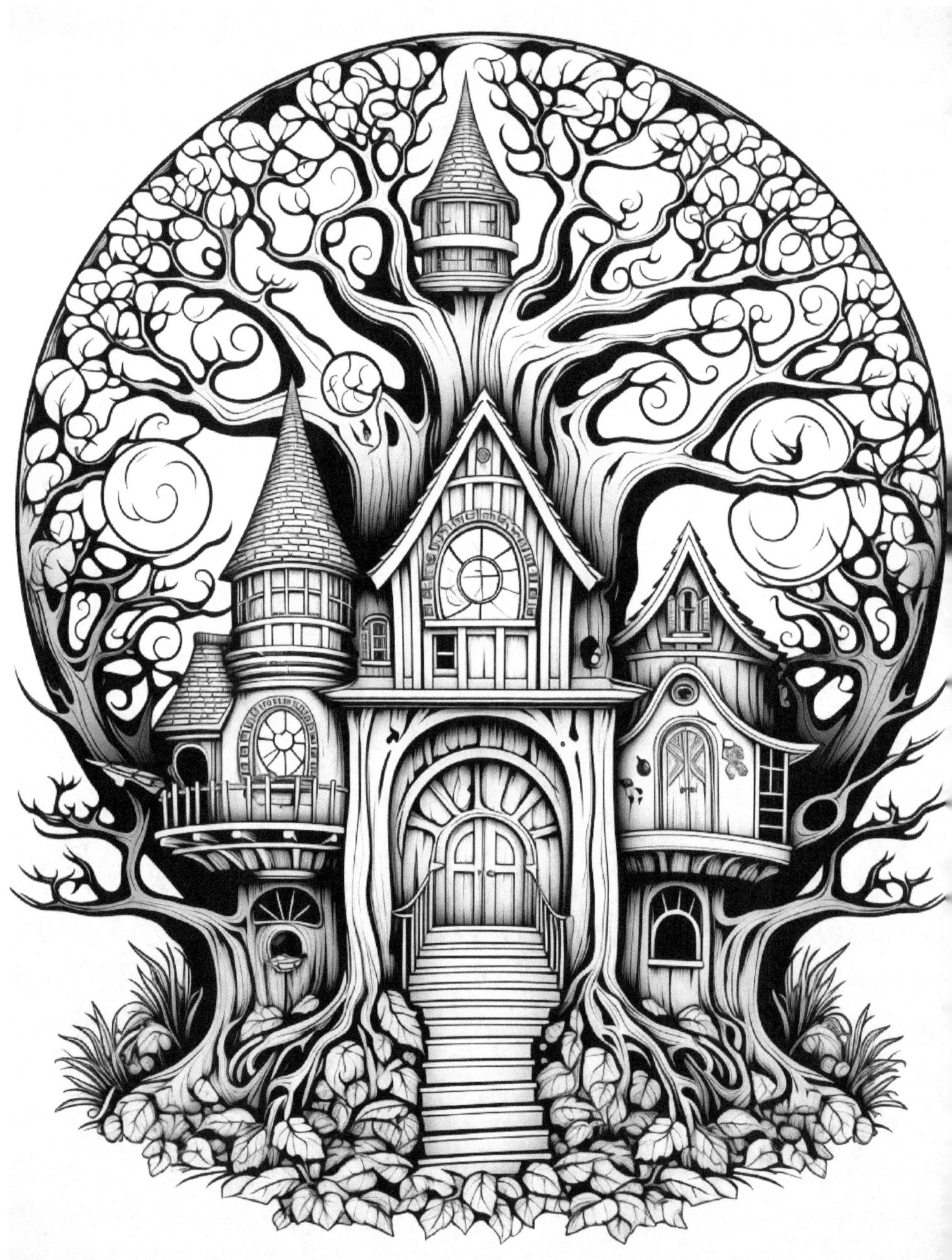

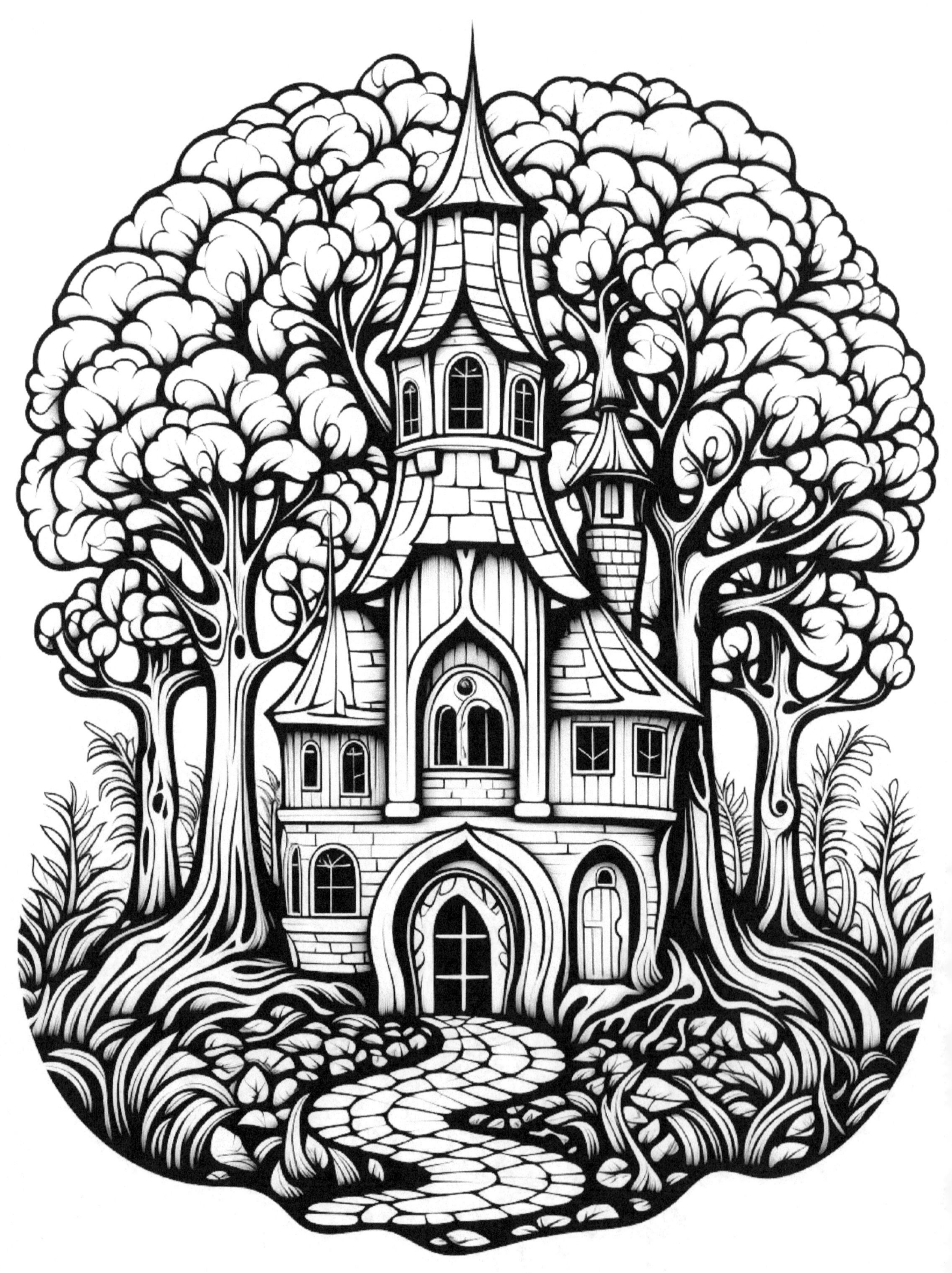

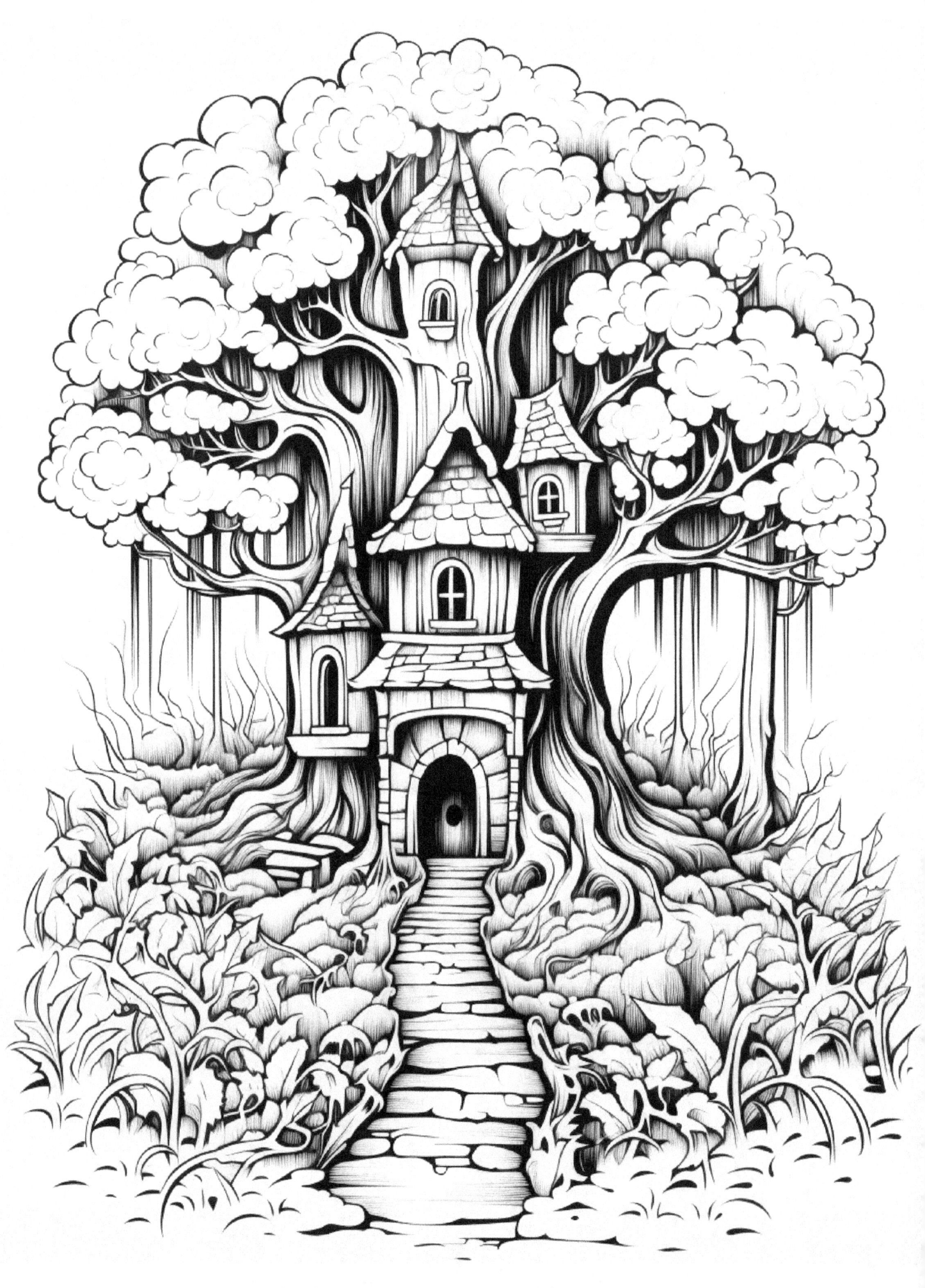

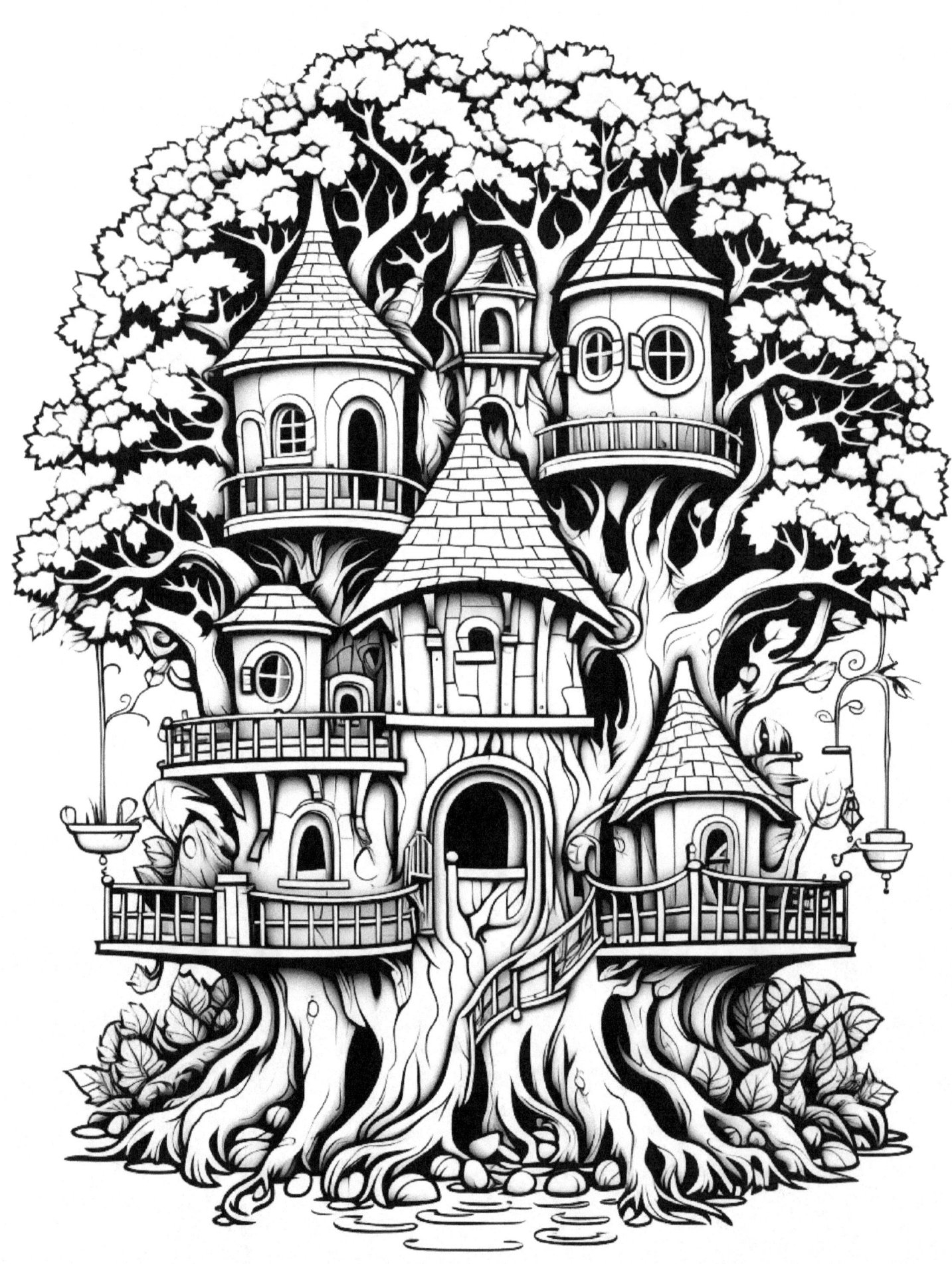

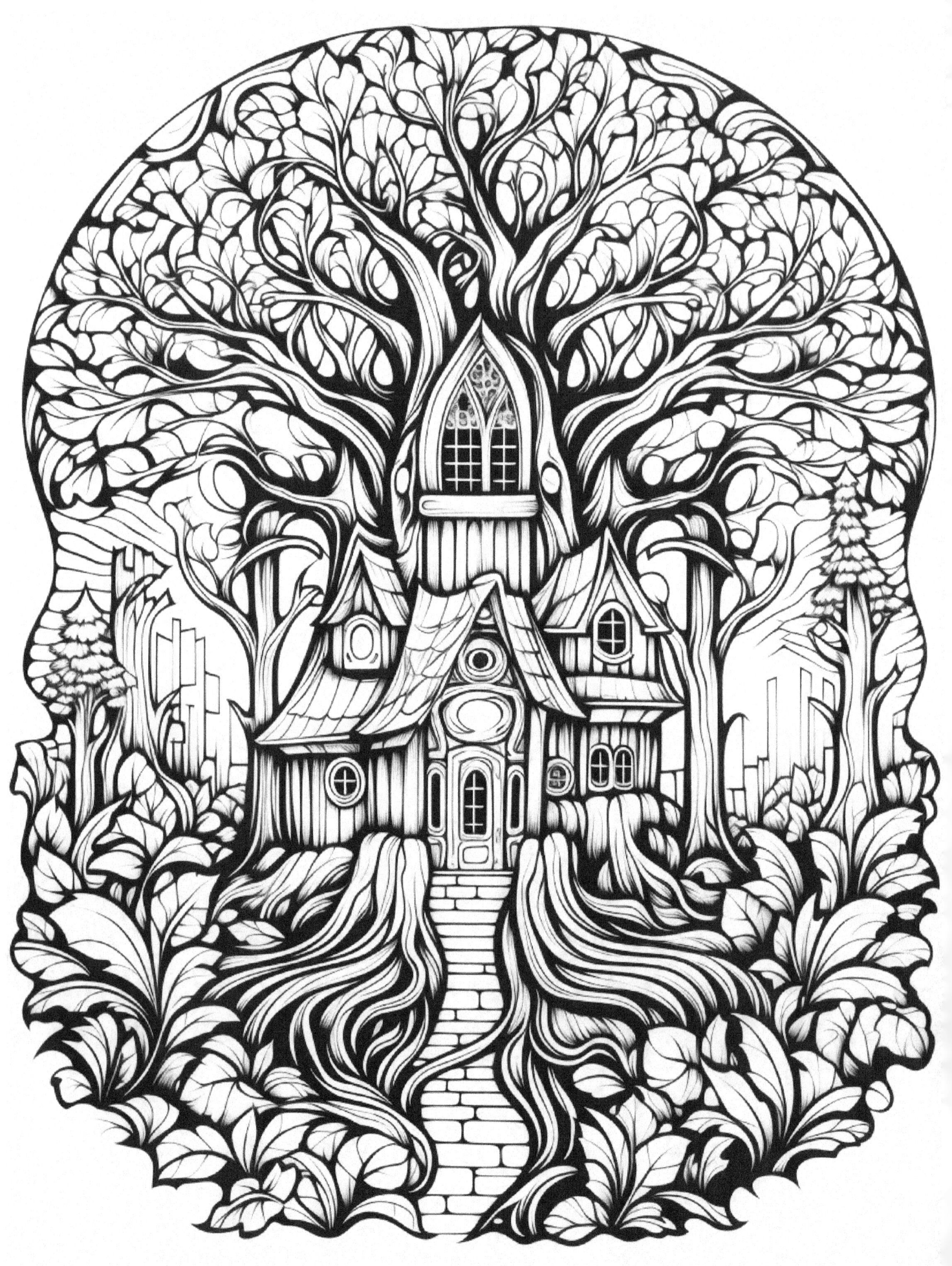

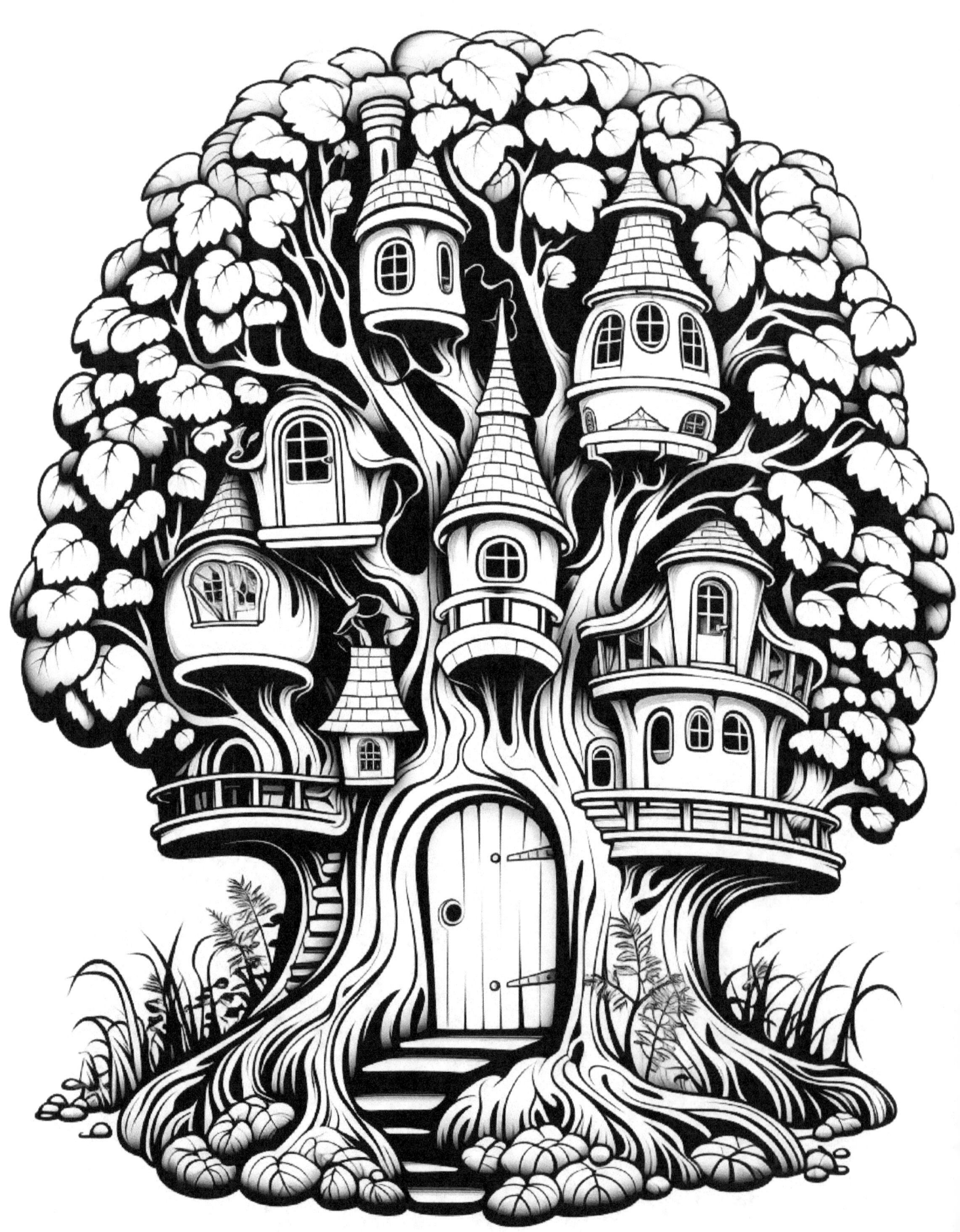

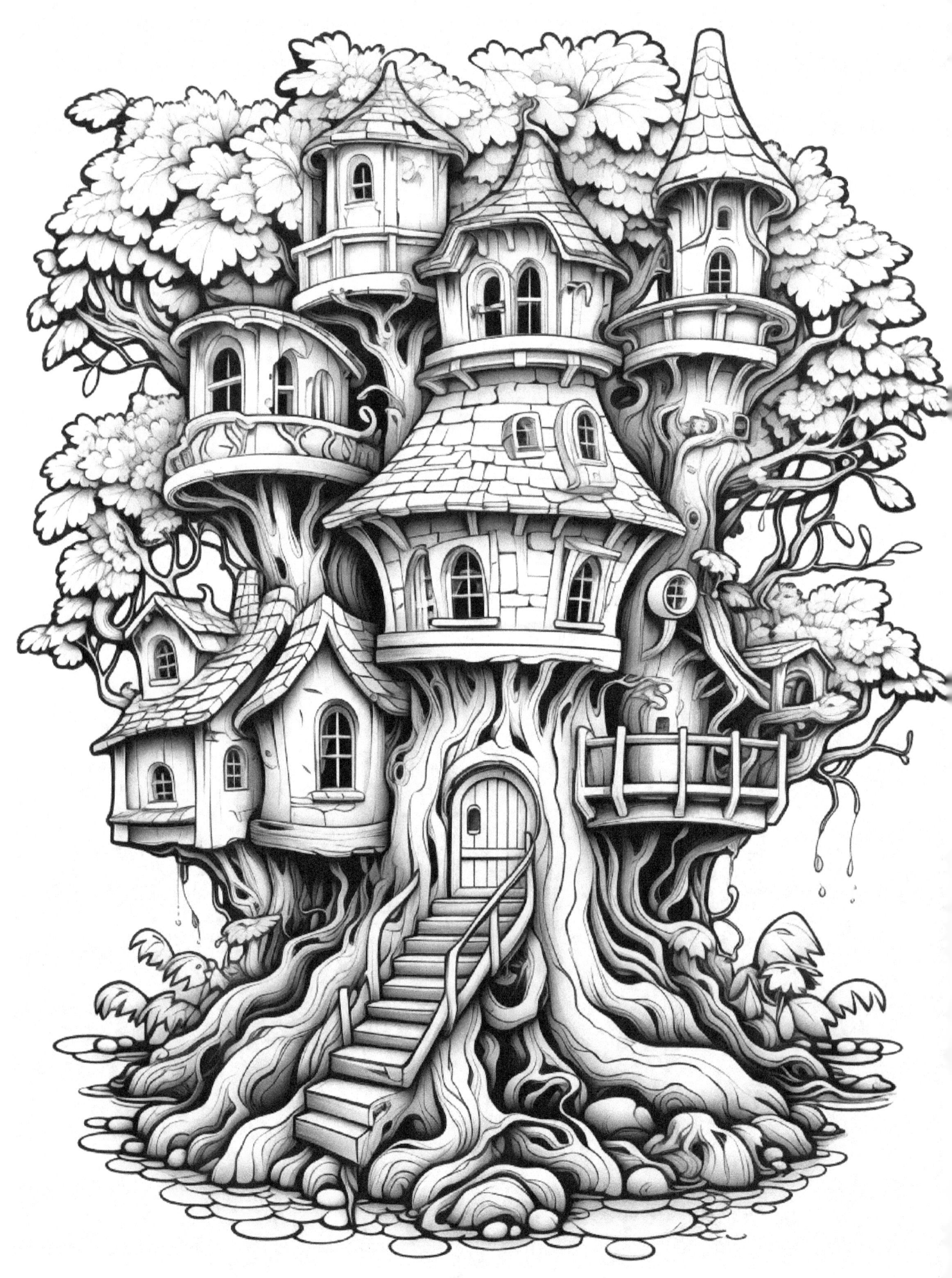

*Scan Me*

*More books from our collection*

Al&Vy
Published

We appreciate you selecting our book, buying our coloring book, and helping our tiny business.

We wish you joy when coloring! We thank all of the contributors to this book for their generosity.

On our Amazon website, kindly post a review and some of your lovely colored photos.